Preparation for His Presence

Min. Que. Payne

iUniverse, Inc.
New York   Bloomington

Preparation for His Presence

The views expressed in this work are solely those of the author and do not necessarily reflect the views of the publisher, and the publisher hereby disclaims any responsibility for them.

iUniverse books may be ordered through booksellers or by contacting:

iUniverse
1663 Liberty Drive
Bloomington, IN 47403
www.iuniverse.com
1-800-Authors (1-800-288-4677)

Because of the dynamic nature of the Internet, any Web addresses or links contained in this book may have changed since publication and may no longer be valid.

ISBN: 978-1-4502-1562-6 (sc)
ISBN: 978-1-4502-1566-4 (ebk)

Printed in the United States of America

iUniverse rev. date: 3/16/2010

Introduction

The purpose, predestined idea and vision of this book is to give insight and inspiration as to the purpose and empowerment of your praise, worship, and your leadership before God's people. It was designed by the Holy Spirit and penned to give you a map and a model to use allowing your praise, be it dancing, singing, music, prophetic flow, intercession, or even the preached word, to go to another level in Him. Preparation for His Presence is a workout in the worship. It is a book written through an experience of worship and the idea to share the knowledge and wisdom revealed to me during that time of study, and meditation. Preparation for His Presence is a mandate that He has given us all for His glory to fill the earth, and His people. The question is are we obeying the command and fulfilling the word, or are we performing in the task, and not pursuing the truth and reality of the assignment with honor and humility? They that worship Him, must worship Him in spirit and in truth (*John 4:24*). In other words, is your worship for real?

As you are reading and meditating on the word allowing the Holy Spirit to speak to you. Consider this, if praise is what you do, then allow it to sore to heights unknown. At the end of every chapter or session as we call it, there is space provided to journal your experience, your thoughts, your time of meditation and revelation.

(I Cor.2:9-13) but as it is written, Things which eye saw not, and ear heard not, and which entered not into the heart of man, Whatsoever things God prepared for them that love him.

But unto us God revealed them through the Spirit: for the Spirit searcheth all things, yea, the deep things of God. For who among men knoweth the things of a man, save the spirit of the man, which is in him? even so the things of God none knoweth, save the Spirit of God. But we received, not the spirit of the world, but the spirit which is from God; that we might know the things that were freely given to us of God.

Which things also we speak, not in words which man's wisdom teacheth, but which the Spirit teacheth; combining spiritual things with spiritual words.

Though the Lord gave us the assignment to write this book, the Holy Spirit is the true author, teacher, and revealer of all truth. The preparation season, is being fit for the Master's use, positioned for His presence, and prepares us for a close encounter to be able to seek His face. In other words this is a workout in worship the Lord himself has called you to. As you read consider the things that are a hinderance in our lives, ailments, illnesses, doubt, fear, sometimes just plain and simple lack of trust in what and who the Father calls you. Seek the Lord and open yourself up to receive the purpose and design as to why this book in this season.

Prepare to Enter in the Holy Place of His presence. Prepare to enter in another dimension of the spirit of who He is in you. This is a season of necessity for empowerment, enlightenment, and endowment.

Dedication

To Craig, the love of my life, thank you for your obedience and confirming the word of the Lord on that awesome night in our home. Thank you for your support, love, prayers, and encouragement. You are my gift for life from the Lord. Thank you for choosing me to be your good thing.

To my boys D'Andre, and Dante you are my joy and anointed ones. You are both men of valor and God's choice, always choose and acknowledge Him in all your ways.

Mommy, you and Daddy showed me the love and word of the King through your love and compassion for each other. Mom, though Dad is no longer with us, our love for him binds us all together forever in this life and the life hereafter. Without pushing and challenging me to live to the standard of the Master as the choice for my life where would I be.

Daddy thank you for always challenging me to live the word and not just read and study it. I so admired the diligent way you served, loved, taught and studied the word of God. I love you and miss you terribly.

I vow to always remember your words of love, encouragement, and commitment to the Lord and the legacy you left us to carry on as a doer of the word.

To my Pastor, Apostle H.Daniel Wilson and Pastor Mom Beverly L Wilson, you both have shown your sons and daughters of Valley Kingdom Ministry International and those around the world, the word of God living and alive that propels us all endlessly in the presence of the Lord to long for him for a glory to glory worship experience. Thank you for being you, my spiritual parents. You are second to none.

SGM (KSE), and FHG you are the absolute best, all my love and honor to each of you.

Contents

"Getting Prepared"

Let's begin by sharing with you how this book came about.

One night while I was watching a program on a Christian channel about worship and how does that look. My husband and my son were in another room watching the same program. The woman on the television was pointing at the camera saying will you say 'yes' and I said to myself, I have said, yes. Again she said, just open your mouth and say yes again. I did just that and felt transcended as if time where I was paused and only the voice of the Lord mattered and moved. The Lord said to me, abandon yourself and worship me, then you can demonstrate the position of my presence. While the Lord was dealing with me in the den of our home he was telling my husband, "Tell my daughter if she will say yes, write the book they will know, the position of praise, and the access to worship me in the Holy place. My husband and my son quickly put together what the Lord had given to my husband in the form of what is now the book cover you hold in your hand, and I kept the original letter he wrote to me. He did not speak this to me, the Lord told him to write it down.

Now, don't miss this!! The Lord was telling him upstairs what the results of my obedience to saying yes downstairs would avail. God has a way of working everything out for you good, but for His Glory.

This manual and that is exactly what this book is, will give you biblical understanding, equipping, stirring, and opportunity to submit yourself holy and acceptable unto God, which is the only way to serve him, and your reasonable service. This is the only way that the Lord will accept your praise. His word says that, "we must come to him with a pure heart, to praise him, any other way your praise is polluted. I pray that this manual will give you insight and understanding by the leading, guiding and direction of the Holy Spirit as to how God has structured your praise, and worship unto him.

This is a seven chapter manual. Seven is the number of completion. The Holy Spirit gave this manual as a guide not a bible; however it will give biblical instructions as to the purpose of your praise. If praise is what you do, and you want your praise personally, and corporately in your church, your ministry, and your home for that matter to be founded on the power and press of the Holy Spirit, Grab hold to what the Lord is saying to you as to why he had you to select this material to read.

So I would like to begin with a prayer and declaration that you must say out loud, so if you are not in a place that you can experience, and receive the full visitation of the Holy Spirit and the activation that it will set off in your spirit man, I suggest you stop and wait until you are in such a place. Throughout this manual you will have several visitations from the Holy Spirit, because again I am reminding you that this manual was birthed out of worship, and intimate time in the Master's face. With that said here we go.

Prayer & Declaration

LORD I THANK YOU AND BLESS YOUR HOLY AND RIGHTEOUSNESS NAME, FOR YOU ARE A MIGHTY AND JUST GOD, AND WORTHY OF ALL THE PRAISE AND ADORATION. I LIFT UP YOUR NAME, THE SOVREIGN GOD OF THE ENTIRE UNIVERSE. YOU ARE THE GOD OF ALL CREATION, AND I THANK YOU FOR ALL THAT YOU CREATED ME TO BE AS AN INSTRUMENT OF PRAISE, A WORSHIPPER, A CONQUEROR, AND AN OVERCOMER, AND VICTORIOUS. YOU CREATED ME IN YOUR IMAGE AND LIKENESS, AND PLACE THE DEPTH OF YOUR WORD IN THE INWARD PART OF MY HEART. LORD CREATE IN ME A CLEAN HEART AND RENEW THE RIGHT SPIRIT WITHIN ME THAT I MAY WORSHIP YOU IN SPIRIT AND IN TRUTH. LORD I PRESENT MYSELF TO YOU AS A VESSEL SAYING YES TO ALL THAT YOU WANT TO STIR, ACTIVATE, AND IGNITE IN ME TO PRAISE YOU WITH A HUNGER, AND THIRST. LONGING FOR RIGHTEOUSNESS THAT ONLY BEING IN YOUR PRESENCE CAN QUENCH. FATHER I SURRENDER MY MIND, MY INTELLECT, MY BODY, MY BEING WHICH IS IN YOU, AND MY STRENGTH. SHOW ME THE DEPTH OF YOUR GOOD PLEASURE IN MY PRAISE THAT I MAY ENTER INTO

A NEW REALM WITH YOU IN WORSHIP. LORD BID ME COME INTO THAT SECRET PLACE WITH YOU TO EXPERIENCE YOU LIKE I HAVE NEVER HAD BEFORE. FATHER I DRAW NIGH UNTO YOU THAT YOU MAY DRAW NIGH UNTO ME.

FATHER I PRAISE YOU WITH ALL OF MY STRENGTH, ALL OF MY MIGHT, BECAUSE I AM DESPERATE FOR YOU. LORD I NEED TO KNOW YOU IN THE FULL POWER OF YOUR RESURRECTION. I WANT TO KNOW YOU LIKE DAVID, A MAN AFTER YOUR HEART, LIKE MOSES A MAN YOU CAME AND SPOKE TO AND COMMUNED WITH. LORD I OPEN MYSELF TO YOU RIGHT NOW. COME INTO MY HEART AND MY PRAISE TO INHABIT IT FOREVER. CHANGE MY MIND TO THAT OF CHRIST THAT I MIGHT GAIN THE WISDOM AND BLESSING TO WORSHIP YOU AS THE ANGELS IN HEAVEN HAVE THE OPPORTUNITY TO DO.

COME IN LORD TOUCH MY MIND THAT I MIGHT GAIN UNDERSTANDING OF YOUR WORD WITH REVELATION AND ILLUMINATION. TOUCH MY BODY THAT I MIGHT MOVE AND ACT

IN OBEDIENCE TO WHAT YOU REVEAL TO ME. CAUSE MY ENTIRE BEING TO RESPOND AS AN ACT OF OBEDIENCE WITH THE ACTIVITY OF MY LIMBS. GIVE ME CREATIVE IDEAS AND KNOWLEDGE TO PRESENT YOU WITH PRAISE THAT WILL GET YOUR ATTENTION, AND CAPTURE YOUR HEART, AND BE PLEASING TO YOU TO LOOK UPON AND INHABIT IN JESUS NAME.

JESUS I GIVE YOU FULL ACCESS TO ALL THAT I AM ALL THAT I HAVE. JESUS ARISE IN ME BY THE STIRRING OF THE SPIRIT MAN IN ME.

I REPENT NOW OF ALL OF MY SINS, AND MY INIQUITIES.

I RECOGNIZE AND ACKNOWLEGE YOU DIED ON THE CROSS FOR ME. I REPENT AND NOW ASK FOR YOUR FORGIVENESS FOR NOT DISPLAYNG AN ATTITUDE, AND CHARACTER THAT PLEASES YOU. I THANK YOU FOR BEING A JUST AND FAITHFUL GOD TO FORGIVE ME OF ALL THAT I HAVE SAID, DONE , AND THOUGHT THAT WAS NOT IN ACCORDANCE WITH YOU WORD.

I DECLARE THAT YOUR NAME WILL BE LIFTED UP. I DECLARE JESUS THAT I WILL LIFT UP YOUR NAME AND GIVE YOU GLORY, HONOR, AND PRAISE. I DECLARE THAT MY PRAISE AND DISPLAY OF MY ADORATION AND EXALTATION OF YOU IN PRIVATE AND IN PUBLIC WILL BE PURE. I WILL LIVE HOLY. I WILL LIVE AND SEEK AFTER YOUR KINGDOM AND YOUR RIGHTEOUSNESS, TO HONOR YOU AND LIVE IN CONTINOUS PURSUIT OF YOUR HEART. TO YOU BE GLORY, POWER, HONOR, AND ALL THE EXALTATION IS YOURS IN THE PRECIOUS AND MATCHLESS NAME OF MY LORD, MASTER, SAVIOR AND REDEEMER, JESUS CHRIST.

AMEN

"NOW TAKE SOME TIME AND WORSHIP AND BE STILL SO HE CAN REVEAL SOME THINGS TO YOU"

Session I
Chosen to Change

As you begin this journey I must warn and challenge you at the same time. You, the vessel must avail every part of your being to this process if you are really going to enter this preparation season seriously. Someone may be depending on you to carry it through to the end.

Throughout this journey we will refer to the word of God which is the foundation and true road map for our lives. Study the passages, and scriptures for life application and not just a point of information.

You are the vessel that the Lord desires to use, and that requires some work. In order to be a vessel the Master can use to display the beauty of His holiness in your praise, you must be purified and made whole. Sometimes after being in a position for a while, or responsible for something for so long we get complacent, and it becomes the norm and second nature to us. We can do it without thinking because we are that familiar it and use to the functional operation of the position.

Have you ever been driving somewhere and get there and not remember how. It's a route you always take so you don't have to think about. Well, that is sometimes how we operate in the roll of leader and the one held responsible for the leading of God's people into His presence is a position not to be taken lightly. We sing without thought or much effort, dance, and move and rely on our talent and not the anointing. It becomes the thing we do and not what we are. We only turn it on when required before others, and not a daily practice or lifestyle. The truth of the matter is we have become so familiar with the position that we have neglected the preparation and passionate pursuit we use to run after God with and the honor of serving Him in the office and purpose of our position we still hold only by grace.

We will get into God's original purpose and strategy of the place we operate in called praise and worship be it leaders, psalmist, minstrels, minister of dance and movement, etc. God set a particular people aside to set the atmosphere of worship before him.

There was a purpose, position and power they were given just to please the King of kings. We do what we do in that operation or position and never really think about it anymore, not realizing what it could cost us. We take on a Queen Vashti persona and character (see the book of Esther for more details and background).

Well let's look at an individual who was chosen along with a few others to begin a season of preparation for cleansing and purification to replace someone who lost sight and perspective of the honor they had.

Let's look at Esther who was a young girl chosen by the king's mandate for his servants to go in the town and select the young women of that area to come to the king's court. They were afforded this opportunity after the current queen (Vashti) was removed from her position due to a lack of respect for the king.

Just as Esther and the others were prepared for a year or more to become a queen, so must you be for the King of kings. She was bathed in fine oils and spices, and set aside for special preparation to be summoned before his presence (the king) at an appointed time. Although there were several young women being prepared, Esther somehow stood out, and was given preferential treatment and favor. The Holy Spirit would have you to know that you could not do what you are about to do before now because the timing was not right and he could not have you expose yourself or display you to the world too soon because it may have destroyed you or the purpose that he birthed in you before the beginning of time. But, now is the acceptable time, so get ready!!!

Esther was also not arrogant and put no thought on herself. She thought more of the people she represented than herself. In Esther 2:10, Mordecai instructed her (Esther) not to reveal her people or family, at least not yet. For so long you have said why them and not me, why does it seem as though you use and hear everyone else except me Lord, why can't I get close to you Lord to hear your voice like others do, and feel your touch in such an intimate way. He has chosen you, and set you aside for RIGHT NOW, THIS IS YOUR SEASON AND YOUR TIME!!!!! ARE YOU READY?

Remember in the book of Esther chapter 2 verse 12 all the young virgins were prepared and bathed in oil of myrrh for six months and then six months in fine perfumes. The oils were used to cleanse and prepare them as well as equip the vessel from the inside. This process, using the myrrh oil had medicinal as well as natural purpose. It was a detoxifying system that purified, healed and helped the vital organs of the body from a natural perspective. From a spiritual perspective it was used as a preparation for a religious ceremony. Has the Lord begun pouring His oil on you and what has it healed, purified, or cleansed?

Have you forgiven those that have despitefully used you? Have you humbled yourself to the shepherd of the house you are suppose to serve under. Have you submitted your gift to the ministry the Lord has called you to? In other words can they smell the oil of change on you? Are you healthy and made whole from within because you have let the oil of the Master heal and set you free? The King is calling for and preparing His queen "you". The King wants you whole not just holy.

The perfumes were used to prepare her on the outside. This process was and will always be a part of the preparation season for anyone that the Lord chooses. We must be willing to go through our own cleansing and detoxification process. The Holy Spirit would have me to say that they both must be appealing to the King, meaning the inside and out. If you are beautiful on the outside and you attitude, or character is not, then you are still not ready. The King's attraction to us will be by what He senses and not just by what He sees. We must be appealing by scent (your praise), and senses (your heart). If you have a great character and integrity but you don't take care of yourself, then know that you are still not ready.

Do you not know that your body is a temple of the Holy Spirit, who is in you, whom you have received from God? You are not your own; you were bought at a price. Therefore honor God with your body. (I Cor.6:19-20)

Your preparation time and season is designed to prepare you for the King to display His beauty and image of His own likeness. Desire all that he has given you on the inside and outside to be revealed. But make no mistake He looks past the flesh, he searches the heart and intention thereof.

Our God is Spirit and they that worship him must do so in spirit and in truth (John 4:24).

God is looking for a people and a temple (you) that he can dwell in the mist of and move through. We must be a prepared people for a King.

The church (you) are the vessel that the Lord is seeking for. We are living in the Davidic order and times. God is rebuilding the tabernacle of

(Amos 9:11). He spoke of this being the temple or place where he would dwell, and inhabit forever *(I Kings 9:3)*.

Rev. 21:3 says, And I heard a great voice out of heaven saying, Behold, the tabernacle of God is with men and he will dwell with them, and they shall be his people, and God himself shall be with them, and be their God.

In order to be that temple where He will dwell forever, some things get worked out in the worship, and the preparation season of refinement is a season of necessity. You don't want the King to come to you by the aroma of your vessel (your praise, and your presentation), only to find that the inner workings are of no real substance, quality or value. He wants you to operate with power, and authority.

And for those that would say I cannot relate, that is not my story, hold on we will come down your street, ring your bell, or find the key under the flower pot that the Holy Spirit knows you hid for just such an occasion as this. Now some may say I have done all that and still I have no access. I have been preparing and living right before God and still nothing.

Well David's experience was God downloaded the architectural plans for the tabernacle into him (David); however Solomon, David's son was given the permit and permission by God to build it.

Now, although, Solomon built the tabernacle, his father David, was the king at the time who really desired to build the tabernacle. However David told him (Solomon), he was chosen by God to build it. Solomon had no desire or understanding of what to do or how to get started. The Father (God) gave David by divine design blueprints, and all the specifics for construction. David obeyed God by releasing the plans to his son Solomon. David called on the people to lend unto Solomon all the materials, expertise in skill, and support to accomplish the goal. The Lord may give you the vision and even allowed you to write the plan, but could you release it to someone else to fulfill the purpose in the vision or relinquish your position? Could you give it your all, and rejoice anyhow?

God wants to inhabit the praises of His people, however the praise must be pure and the purpose of the praise must be real and not have a personal agenda fulfilled. We cannot offer Him that which cost us nothing. Sometimes the thing we must offer God is our own desire, plan and agenda. David offered God his obedience and his worship by saying yes to His will. Could we say that we would so easily do the same?

Would you release the vision and plan even if it cost you a reputation, thoughts or perspective of your position? God sometimes gives you as a gift to another to submit your all to the cause of another. Could you allow someone less qualified by your standards to go forth, yielding your all and submitting to the person chosen? Is that the way you feel now in ministry, on the job, in life? Are you the better singer, dancer, musician, exhorter, yet someone else less skilled or trained has the lead position.

To go before the King you must come a certain way. The presence of the King and the audience of the King require something from you first.

"Who may ascend into the hill of the Lord? Or who may stand in His holy place? He who has clean hands and a pure heart. (Ps.24:3-4)

We cannot go before the Father or be used to display his glory, without first going through the process. We must seek him, purify our hearts, cleanse our hands, pick up, clean up, and clear up any and all portions and parts of our lives that could prevent us from the position of praise, or the right to operate in power to set the atmosphere for someone else to freely worship him. Some of this cleansing process will be by prayer, some by fasting, some by deliverance, but all by sanctification.

II Cor. 16:11-18 is a reflection and gage by which the chosen of the Lord Jesus Christ should set their thermometer. Take some time, pray and meditate on this passage of scripture and earnestly seek the Lord on the application of this word to your life.

PLEASE DON"T SAY THAT THIS DOES NOT APPLY TO YOU!!!! ALL HAVE SINNED AND COME SHORT OF THE GLORY. Allow the Holy Spirit to reveal what truth and place to apply the hand of God to work on you. (This may be a good time to journal some things)

Ask yourself theses questions;

- Why do I want the attention of the King?

- What do I want from the King?
- What will I do with what I want?

When we seek the attention of the King, just as Esther did, it was not for her personal gain. She was chosen and prepared for a season, and then presented. It was then that the king saw and gave her an invitation into his inner courts and spoke to her and offered her what he had. Has the King given you a personal invitation into the inner courts? We are all a prepared people for a prepared King, but has he noticed you by the scent of your praise?

There is a protocol and an order by which we must follow to come before the King. Esther was a beautiful girl and set up to be a blessing to an entire nation of people. God has chosen and predestined you for a purpose greater than yourself, and not for personal gain or fame.

What if Esther had decided she was good enough for the king as she was, relying on her beauty and gifts alone, and not allowed the preparation season and the circumstances of her purpose to be fully developed? What if David the king had said to the people God told me and chosen me to build the tabernacle? What command and thing has God given you and are you following His direction or your own hearts decision? There is a time and a season to everything. Allow the season and timing of God to align and present the purpose of all things.

Read, pray and wait for understanding of the passage of scripture *Romans 8:28-30*. This is a key passage for those whom God has chosen to use at this time, and season. We all have purpose and he has need of all that is in you for such a time as this. The King has asked for you, now you are being prepared to be presented. When we put the interest of the Kingdom above ourselves then God gets the glory and His people get the victory. I like to describe it as a lack of self preservation for the good of the preservation of the kingdom and His people. It can cost you and it will and so it should.

Seek ye first the kingdom of God and His righteousness, and He will add all other things to you. (Matt. 6:33)

We are not to offer him that which cost us nothing. If what we are offering up cost you nothing, as if it were the old something in your closet you just happen to have and want to give to Him as if He would not know where you got that from, I advise you to be careful. Our praise should be and is required to be pure. We can only come before Him according to Psalm 24:4, *"He who has clean hand and a pure heart"*. Our praise must be pure and without blemish, this does not mean perfect. He wants what we have to come from our heart with full understanding that He knows the intent of the heart.

This is a good time to come before the Father and allow the cleansing process to go even deeper, if it hasn't already. If the vessel(you) have anything in it that will cause the purity of your praise to be hindered, blocked, or tainted in any way, take the time and go through the bathing process of the holy spirit to take place now.

The Holy Spirit will show you where the real cleansing of the most hidden things is. The Holy Spirit comes to reveal all truth to us about who we are, what we are not, and directs us into the who, what, and why God has called us into himself.

Romans 12:1 says *Therefore, I urge you brothers(this is not gender related), in view of God's mercy, to offer your bodies as living sacrifices, holy and pleasing to God-this is your spiritual act to worship.*

Our preparation season is a time of fasting and praying, not just for cleansing but also to get a clearer ear to hear from the Lord. How can we follow Him accept we know His voice. While Esther was in the courts going through her process she was not just being prepared as all the other virgins were being prepared but she found favor with every official in the courts. She was chosen by the king's courts men, but to fulfill a purpose greater than herself, she found favor with the King of kings. Even the selection and location of her quarters from the king's men and eunuchs in the courts put her within sight distance from where the king spent time. She received the best of everything, including housing. During the entire process she resided closest to where the king dwelt. As she was being prepared for the king she was also being set up to be presented by the King (our Lord) for His people. Even the king when he saw her was taken by her. Has the King taken special interest in you? What about you have captured the heart of the King?

I would imagine that during this process, she may have had a few questions. But nowhere in the word of God does it say she complained, however due to her submission to the process, I would imagine her character and demeanor of humility granted her a position of favor over all the other young women selected and experiencing the same process . Have you put your survival in the hands and care of the Holy Spirit for real? The King could make one command and have you removed from His courts, even before the time and season of your being presented comes. Let humility, honor, and meekness keep you in the courts long enough to be presented.

Queen Vashti took her position in the courts to a level that displeased the king and even his court. It was established that she should never be allowed to come before the king again.

What if because of arrogance, and vanity the King never allowed you to come before his presence again? Ask yourself this, is my praise for him just to get me a place in the courts, or is it to build up the kingdom because I want to praise him because of who he is to me and through me? Take a moment and go before the King with praise on your lips for no less than 5 minutes.

If it can't get the King's attention, and the interest of the courts, take it to another level beyond the one you are currently in. Your praise should take you outside the realm of your own existence, and draw you into a selfless place, called the inner courts.

This is a place of provocation that the King escorts you into. The perfumes and oil's aroma can and does get His attention and captures Him. You become intriguing, interesting and a delight in His presence. Not just to look upon but to have in His presence by your presentation (praise, adoration, exhortation, etc.).

The praise from your lips should interest Him enough, to hold His attention because it describes Him, it draws Him in like a sweet invoking fragrance that He wants more of. It touches a place in Him that was already connected to you. Your every intention is reverencing Him for who he is, not just for what He can do for you.

Allow this understanding to continuously draw you in deeper and deeper. It will cause you to have the Master's full attention. You must forget about you, and solely, focus on the King. Let the oil in your lantern fill the wick of your heart to ignite a fire, a passion, a sincere hunger for His presence until it becomes impossible to do without daily.

That will and must become the position of you gate entry praise, and His inner court invitation. Design it so that it becomes a full expression of you love and adoration for Him. You cannot enter the gates without an invitation, or a just cause to see the King. Remember the questions we asked earlier about your need and purpose of getting the King's attention, well the guards at the gates are Spirit and Truth.

Your answer to these questions must line up with these two guards, or you will not gain access. Seek the King for justifiable reasons, and not just to be seen in the courts, or even to carry the invitation around to show it off. For example, don't go around saying you are a minister of dance, or the gospel, or boast of a title or position, and have no fruit to show. Don't embellish the truth about what you do or the responsibilities of that position. Let your truth and your invitation cast off the spirit of the Master to be true to the Master. So often we flaunt a position so others may see our power in that position (authority). God gives position in the courts and the body so that they may edify, build up, or set the body to fitly be joined together.

No matter what the position or the posture is, it must all reflect the purpose of the King in the end. Queen Vashti had a position, and when she boasted to high of herself, and thought more highly of herself than she ought to and refused the kings command she was released of her title, her position, and her authority. Her position was revoked and she was ultimately replaced. The same thing happened to Satan, remember he was the praise and worship leader. God put everything in him that pleased Him the father. Satan looked at himself as equal to, as or greater than the creator. He decided he liked the attention for himself and because he thought too much of himself he got kicked out of heaven. You and I have replaced him. His intentions is not necessarily that of a desire to get his original position back, he just wants to keep you and I from being in that position. We have the awesome privilege, and honor to be that sweet sound unto the Master's ear, and the sweet savor or smell that pleases the Master's pallet. Let the character of your life and the determinations in your heart reflect the light of praise to illuminate His glory through all that you do.

Our purpose by the Creator is to create an atmosphere that is filled with His praise, adoration, and worship. So it is in heaven, so let it be on earth.

This honor due all the saints according to the word of God. Psalms 149 and 150 speaks of the why, and the what when we praise Him.

We must understand the purpose of our position, as well as the process to get us there. Gaining position in His presence should not be predicated in or on the present or gift in His hand to give you. Praise is the display of your thanks and heart of gratitude just for who he is. Praise is an acknowledgement of His greatness, His kindness, His out pouring of love, grace, mercy, and goodness towards us. Your praise should reflect your heart, whether that is in song, dance, music, or simply verbal communication. Our hearts of thanksgiving, lavishing of praise and adoration on the Master gets His attention to ask you, or in most cases gives you what you don't even ask for from Him. This reaches far beyond the measure of our ability to think or even imagine. Remember, eyes have not seen, nor ears heard, neither has it entered in the imagination of man, the thing that God hath planned for us. He wants our hearts to be willing and our flesh subject to the spirit. We are counted as sheep for the slaughter; this does not mean that we are easy targets for the enemy to pick off. However, even as Christ was as innocent as a lamb and willing to be a sacrifice and a gift for the salvation of the world, so must we be the work of the King and the Kingdom, as Queen Esther did when she said "well if I parish, I parish". The same requirement is placed upon us for the good of the Kingdom. We must allow our flesh to die and become subject to the spirit. Let our pride die, our agendas die, our vanity die, or need for attention, and recognition must die. Take a few minutes and be still and let the Holy Spirit reveal what and where the next level of cleansing process needs to dig deeper. Again only those with clean hands and pure heart are allowed to come before the King.

We should not play games, or hide that most secret thing from the hand of the Holy Spirit to work on or work with, remember, God already knows, but the question is will we be real for real? Answer these 3 questions date them and come back and review it later at the half way point of this process. If you can hardly recognize that person as yourself anymore, than, I say to you, well done, and if it looks like not much has changed, then start at this point again, So often we want the progress without a process, shifting or stretching in the process. To grow in grace and in the things of God, there must be a process.

The disciples did not become apostles overnight, yet this was the purpose of the process that they had to progress to. David did not become king overnight, there was a process, and Jabez did not have his territory enlarge without a stretch.

And so we must adhere and submit to the process. We cannot enter into the place and presence of God carrying the things, baggage, and stuff that can have us bound, bothered, or hindered in any way. It is going to cost you. It cost him (Jesus) his life for you. In Psalm 149 is says, *"This honor do all the saints"*. Another way to look at that word saints is chosen and set to a different standard or level of accountability. This is a time of preparation as we enter into His courts with praise. Allow the Holy Spirit to submerge you in the oils that purify and detoxify. The word says let a man examine himself, let a man see his own faults and short comings and then come before the Father broken, and humble. The Holy Spirit can and will interpret even our groans, and cries with intercession. Cry out and be broken for the master to work in, on, and through you.

THIS IS A PROCESS!!!!!!!
Just as a seed is fertilized, and nurtured in the womb of its mother, and the process and gestation period takes time. We must also recognize that the greatness that is in us of the Father also cannot be expected to be developed overnight. We must accept the gestation and fertilization period of our gifts to fully feed and develop from the word of God, by the leading and training of the Holy Spirit.

"Every good gift and every perfect gift comes from above". (James 1:17a)

God knows what gifting he has placed and purposed in you, and when he has perfected the proper season and timing for the unveiling of the gift.

Take some time now and seek the Lord for more clarity for the period of the process you are in, and allow the Holy Spirit to further develop you hearing, understanding, and obedience to what need the Master is fulfilling in you He created for His glory.

Be still and know. To be still is not necessarily mean stop talking and moving. It can mean stop doing what you think is a good idea, and wait for the God idea. Stop doing what you feel you should be doing and wait to hear what the Lord is commanding you to do. Stop trying to fit the Father in what you are doing and find out what the Lord is already in and get in it. We sometimes get so busy doing work in the church and for the church and not realize that God has not sent us to do all of those things at the same time. Busy does not always add up to successful or productive, just busy.

I must work the works of him that sent me, while it is day: the night cometh, when no man can work. John 9:4-5

As long as I am in the world, I am a light to the world. We must "Let our light so shine before men, that they may see our good works, and glorify our Father which is in heaven (Matthew 5:16).

If the ministry or assignment we are in reflects this purpose then ask yourself who's glory through our light are the people we stand before seeing? Give into the process so that the progress of your preparation season reveals His purpose in the end. Be an Esther, or a David for His Glory to be seen in all that you do.

**Challenge

Fast for 24 hours from the thing that would be a sacrifice (television, phone, talking, food, etc.)

Journal your results and revelation

- What is my purpose in this position?

_____
_____
_____
_____
_____
_____
_____
_____
_____
_____

- What is my foundational scripture and why? (Find a scripture that you feel describes your purpose and gift in ministry)

_____
_____
_____
_____
_____
_____
_____
_____
_____
_____

Session II
"Purged, Pruned, Purified, and Processed"

To everything there is a time and a season. The Lord has placed his spirit and justified calling in each of us for a purpose by design. This thing is, the what, when, and the how to display and show forth the character of His glory that He has created and predestined you as the first fruit of his son. You are not a mistake, and Grab hold to this, "HE CREATED YOU FOR HIS GOOD PLEASURE". Your Preparation season has come and you should rejoice and be glad. Some stages of preparation are not pleasant nor do they all feel good, however we are to rejoice in knowing even God himself corrects, chasten, and work on, in and through those he loves. Everything that you are going through or have gone through has not been sent your way by the devil, and his camp. We are the chosen and the elect of God. He is simply establishing the ground work in us for a holy visitation.

Romans 8:14-31
For as many as are led by the Spirit of God, they are the sons of God.

For ye have not received the spirit of bondage again to fear; but ye have received the Spirit of adoption, whereby we cry, Abba, Father.

The Spirit itself beareth witness with our spirit, that we are the children of God:

And if children, then heirs; heirs of God, and joint-heirs with Christ; if so be that we suffer with him, that we may be also glorified together.

For I reckon that the sufferings of this present time are not worthy to be compared with the glory which shall be revealed in us.

For the earnest expectation of the creature waiteth for the manifestation of the sons of God.

For the creature was made subject to vanity, not willingly, but by reason of him who hath subjected the same in hope,

Because the creature itself also shall be delivered from the bondage of corruption into the glorious liberty of the children of God.

For we know that the whole creation groaneth and travaileth in pain together until now.

And not only they, but ourselves also, which have the first fruits of the Spirit, even we ourselves groan within ourselves, waiting for the adoption, to wit, the redemption of our body

For we are saved by hope: but hope that is seen is not hope: for what a man seeth, why doth he yet hope for?

But if we hope for that we see not, then do we with patience wait for it.

Likewise the Spirit also helpeth our infirmities: for we know not what we should pray for as we ought: but the Spirit itself maketh intercession for us with groanings which cannot be uttered. And he that searcheth the hearts knoweth what is the mind of the Spirit, because *he maketh intercession for the saints according to the will of God. And we know that all things work together for good to them that love God, to them who are the called according to his purpose.*

For whom he did foreknow, he also did predestinate to be conformed to the image of his Son, that he might be the firstborn among many brethren.

Moreover whom he did predestinate, them he also called: and whom he called, them he also justified: and whom he justified, them he also glorified.

What shall we then say to these things? If God be for us, who can be against us?

The Holy Spirit is truly the guide into all that the Father has for us and that should be exciting. We must submit to the molding process. In this session allow yourself to be stretched and pulled beyond measure and recognition, to look more like the Master. God has a work for you that must come through you. The Refiner is calling for you to come near the fire. I discovered for myself that, when the Refiner's fire calls for you and hold you in His hand, you feel safe, and secure by the very grip of His hand. I also found out that this fire though very hot and intense can cause the very spirit man in you to simultaneously want to draw closer as your flesh desires greatly to pull away. I asked the Lord how is that possible, and the answer was quite simple. Your flesh can feel the heat, because no flesh shall glory in His presence, and your spirit man only knows and yearns for the fire because it is the part of the Father that feeds and speaks to the most endowed part of your being, your spirit.

Is not my word like as a fire? saith the LORD; and like a hammer that breaketh the rock in pieces?
Jer.23:29) see also Malachi 3:2-4, Mt.3:11, Heb.12:29.

preparation season is one in which the fire of God will come to purify, break, cleanse, and even guard. Be sure that you are really ready for the fire of God. This session is designed to provoke you to fast and pray often. Let the word be your guide, because the Holy Spirit will labor for you as well as cause you to labor for the things of God. The preparation season impregnates you with the anointing that destroys the yoke.

Simply put that thing and even places and things that can and often hinder this process from fully manifesting will be left at the foot of the alter of sacrifice. I declare a freedom from bondage shall overtake you in Jesus name.

"For whom the Son sets free is free indeed".

Seek after the face of God and not just the hand of God. It truly is a greater blessing to be had when you seek after the face of God, then just what comes from His hand. When we seek after His face and hunger for His very presence like the word describes in Matt.6:33 *"Seek ye first the kingdom of God and His righteousness......* As those called to come close, and yes you are called to come close to the Father. You must realize that that is going to require some intimate, face to face time. It will require and command that you come so close that it becomes so much more apparent that the closer you get the less of you that there is to see. Your experience should leave you longing for more and more of Him.

Write down everything that is revealed to you that must be let go. Think of this exercise like cleaning a garden full of weeds, garbage, and junk that is hindering the process for real growth, and fertilization. The Son can't get through to the real ground and seed if all kinds of debris is blocking the way.

Some stuff in the garden seems as though it is o.k. to remain, but make sure you check yourself and determine whether you just like it there, or is it required to be removed because the Lord has another plant (seed) for that space. Some stuff we want to keep and hold on to must GO!!! Be willing to LET GO! Some things will be easier to let go of than others. During and in the preparation season the hardest thing to remove and disconnect from are people, mindsets, and relationships. The thing that keeps us bound and looking through the glass at the promises and promotions of God, are typically the things we think we need to hold on to the most. Take some time once again and seek the Lord on the revelation

of the truth of what is and is not sent from above. Seek the word for foundational support and witness to what you hear in the spirit. At this point you will start developing movement, song, sound and illustration from this new found place in the spirit with the Father. Journaling becomes an important tool from this point forward. Develop a library of music and interpretations of the word including Hebrew and Greek study bibles (Standard, NIV, etc) of the word of God that will become your reference and meditation arsenal.

This is the great time to pause and get in your secret place. It is also advisable to have your journal near. Go ahead; get to a place where you can get into the presence of the Lord. Enter into His gates with thanksgiving and His courts with praise. This is a place that dimensional shifting will and should take place.

Begin with a prayer of thanksgiving and adoration being lavished onto the Father. Allow your spirit man to take over without hindrances and hesitation. Be willing to go before the Father and surrender and reveal all of you flaws and all of your fears. Never forget to be still and quiet and allow this place to be a space that gives the Lord open access to all of you. As we all do we talk so much and listen so little, the Holy Spirit has something to say in regards to our truth, not just our perception of it, but reality of it. Allow some response time, action and activation. The Holy Spirit needs to be your lead and guide. Let the light of the Master direct you footsteps and be willing to step outside of the box of what you know and surrender to the unknown realm in the spirit that was design with you in mind. His mind not yours, His thoughts not yours, His place and space not yours.

This season does come with some quiet time, reflection, and meditation. It could feel like the wilderness. Keep in mind that great power, and purpose was revealed to the Master in His wilderness place. John the Baptist received revelation to prepare the way for the one to come (Jesus) in his wilderness. Be o.k. with a wilderness experience. Be sure to journal, and allow some true time of impartation from the Holy Spirit.

In Romans 8: 22-28(message bible) it reads, *All around us we observe a pregnant creation. The difficult times of pain throughout the world are simply birth pangs. But it's not only around us, it's within us. The Spirit of God is arousing us within. We're also feeling the birth pangs. These sterile and barren bodies of ours are yearning for full deliverance. That is why waiting does not diminish us, any more than waiting diminishes a pregnant mother. We are enlarged in the waiting. We, of course, don't see that what is enlarging us. But the longer we wait, the larger we become, and the more joyful our expectancy. Meanwhile, the moment we get tired in the waiting, God's Spirit is right alongside us helping us along. If we don't know how or what to pray, it doesn't matter. He does our praying in and for us. Making prayer out of our wordless sighs, our aching groans. He knows us far better than we know ourselves, knows our pregnant condition, and keeps us present before God. That's why we can be so sure that every detail in our lives of love for God is worked into something good.*

(Take some time and create and develop a song, sound, or movement with this passage of scripture)

Are you ready to give birth to what God has placed in you from the beginning of time that could only be brought forth RIGHT NOW!!!!

This is a time and a season where things and ideas that the Lord may have given you long ago was designed and predestined to come forth NOW.

Sometimes as Joseph did, we get anxious because God shows us something that is so spectacular and marvelous that we want to snap our fingers and make it happen now, or share and tell too soon, be careful. As we know even as Joseph did, there was and is a process that, if we knew what it would take and the full run of the process we would abandon the project. We do not serve a magician as God, we serve a majestic sovereign King, who knows the plans He has for you, and when they are due to manifest, and they shall.

God has made everything beautiful in its time. The bible tells us to be anxious for nothing, but with prayer and supplication, make your request known. We forget sometimes who is really in charge, and that God is not subject to our needs. God is the Jehovah Jireh, the supplier of our needs, but as it pleases Him, not us. Allow the Holy Spirit to guide you in the truth of every matter, and search you for what is not. God will get His good pleasure out of you, even if it cost you something. If it cost Him to have you, then simply know to reign with Him, we must suffer with Him as well. We should not want to offer Him that which cost us nothing.

God is looking for those He calls His own to present Him in the earth through our lives. The restoration of His bride (us) is now. We must be that generation that will seek His face. We must use every means created by God to show forth His glory. Dance, music, sound, song, and the spoken word are all tools created by God to display and illuminate His glory. Look at Rev. 4 and Rev. 5, this gives us a brief glimpse of heaven. The word says on earth as it is in heaven, the kingdoms of this world must become the kingdom or systems of our Lord. The industry or system of this world that seems to be capturing the minds, will, and imagination of the people must be turned back to the King. We are a part of the restoration of the temple of David, because God said, that is the only place where He would dwell forever (II Chron. 7:16 and Amos 9:11).

There is a remnant that shall be used to restore and rebuild the tabernacle, and the Lord is awakening and equipping those that are a part of His plan. Can you hear Him calling and saying, arise oh Zion, you sleepers arise.

In the 8th chapter of Romans it really gives a purpose and pre-planned destiny that the Lord has ordained and called into existence before the beginning of time. This season of preparation that we all must process through must be in accordance with the word of God, the call of the Master, and His purpose for the gift. We cannot and should not pursue the dream if it is not God inspired. Sometimes, we seek after the dream, and watch it become our nightmare, if the Lord has not ordained it. Your dance, songs, music, and even literary writings must be biblically sound, and Holy Spirit guided. What is He saying to you about the purpose, process, and empowerment of the plans He has for you, and are you listening? As Joseph experienced, there was a reason and purpose bigger than himself that must be fulfilled. Your purpose and what's in you is bigger than you, and for the greater good must be brought out.

If there is a dream or vision the Lord has shown you, trust that it must be fulfilled. And if this is the purpose, and plan of God concerning the gifts he has placed in you, then do what you must do as Christ did. We are the son's or first fruit of the Father that must be *"conformed to the image of His son, the firstborn among many brethren" (Romans 29C.)*

During this preparation season seek the Lord on the process, not the duration of it. Desire and search out the purpose, and not just the position. Yearn for the empowerment and endowment of the anointing that destroys yokes, for His Glory.

As we seek the Lord and the purpose of the gifts that glorify Him and not vanity, and self promotion, then the processing and equipping will begin. He will give us the songs that draw His people into His presence, and set the atmosphere so that His peoples will be free. He will allow us the ability to move in dance that will demonstrate His power. He will let us hear the sounds of heaven that it may be on earth even as it is in heaven. *But we* must be willing to endure the process, even as the Hebrew boys endure the fire so must we be tried and purified by fire, and molded by the potter's hands. What is he requiring of you to let go of to be equipped for the real work, and not just the performance.

Will you say, "Prepare me to be a sanctuary, pure and Holy, tried and true".

Can we honestly surrender let go and let God. God is seeking for face time worshippers. We can no longer operate and pretend to operate with power because the people are dying spiritual, emotionally, and even naturally. Those that are called must awaken and activate the power of the Holy Ghost working in us, on and through to reveal the revelatory knowledge of God to set the people free. We must begin setting true atmospheres of power by the anointing that destroys yokes, bondages, and heaviness off the people of God. This is your purpose for the position, and not a platform for a performance.

Give in to the process for the progress of the Kingdom through you.

Journal question- **"What must you do different to become a vessel for the Master"**

_____
_____
_____
_____
_____
_____
_____
_____
_____
_____

Journal question –**"What has the word of God inspired you to hunger for in becoming this vessel for His use"**

_____
_____
_____
_____
_____
_____
_____
_____
_____
_____

Session III
FIT FOR THE MASTER'S USE

I Cor. 6:19-20
What? know ye not that your body is the temple of the
Holy Ghost which is in you, which ye have of God, and
ye are not your own? For ye are bought with a price:
therefore glorify God in your body, and in your spirit,
which are God's.

God in his infinite wisdom created us in his likeness. He knew what we would be doing on this very day.

In His wisdom, and knowing his creation he gave directions for both the physical man and the spiritual being throughout the bible as to how to take care of both and what not to allow in either parts of our being.

Genesis to revelations speaks of the body as a temple or vessel. So often we allow the situation or circumstances in our lives to dictate the direction or destruction of our temple. In I Cor. 20, it says we are to glorify God in our bodies. God knows and has counted every hair on your head. He knows our dress and pants size. He knows what we are eating and what we're doing with this temple.

This session and purpose is to illuminate the instructions given to us in the word of God as to how to properly take care of the temple that will bring God glory. We will offer God our praise, and will give God worship in our movement and sound while presenting ourselves a living sacrifice Holy and acceptable in his sight to be fit for the Master's use. It is a strategic plan designed by God, directed by the Holy Spirit to Psalm 51:10 our thought process and John 4:24 our purpose in perfecting the temple.

Life's challenges give God opportunity to work through our inability. The father has ordered and ordained some steps for you, and has laid an assignment in its path that is just for you. Our position and accountability is to God. How we take care of what he has given us is an honorable way to show Him your gratitude for the gift.

Our praise is an instrument created by God for his divine connection to us to be able to move through us.

When we raise our hands, wave our arms, clap, jump, sing, and play the instruments, etc., we are initially propelling ourselves into the courts of the father's dwelling place. As we continue and the Holy Spirit moves us deeper into the presence of God our worship catapults us into a place and position in which we receive intimate directions, and guidance.

Psalm100:4 *"Enter into his gates with thanksgiving and into his courts with praise: be thankful unto him, and bless his name.*

The dynamics, purity, and sincerity of your praise has significant impact on God's response to your situation.

They that worship him must worship him in spirit and truth (John 4:24)

When we learn the meaning and purpose of our movement, song, or sound, during our worship we will gain knowledge and power by revelation to overcome greater obstacles. We get an understanding as to why we do things which are out of our norm during the worship experience. For example we leap, or jump in victory instead of curl up and feel defeated in the face of adversity or the middle of the crisis. Or when we clap our hands until they hurt and feel raw, when our flesh wants to say, I quit. Or play a chord that seems out of place that shifts the entire congregation into a time of warfare when a severe spirit of heaviness seemed to have been present.

And as a result of that kind of a release a new song or cry of victory gets released that shatters the walls of imprisonment. So often we are moving or reacting in a certain atmosphere when we hear a certain sound in the mist of praise & worship that seems as though it was a personal direct call to you. That's actually what is happening. The Spirit of God that dwells on the inside of you is responding to God's voice in what you are hearing. The Master is saying I need to use you, I want to talk to you, give me your attention and focus, not the situation or circumstances around you.

Sometimes we can't respond because our flesh is suffering from infirmities, fatigue, worry, shame, doubt, or distractions, and from even being overweight and out of shape. For that reason and the need to get closer to God, we must press pass the flesh, and remember the intent of this session is to illuminate the word to overcome the darkness and bring you into a new place of understanding for strength, authority, and empowerment, so be encouraged.

Today is a new day that you can rejoice and be glad in the Lord, and walk in the divine purpose of God for your life.

Your body or temple is an arsenal that the enemy knows will cause you to walk in victory and not defeat. But as long as he (the enemy Satan) can convince you of what you can't do, he knows he can hold you back for realizing who you really are, and what you really have. You are fearfully and wonderfully made.

You were equipped from the beginning of time with all that you would ever need to be, and that is more than a conqueror, through Christ Jesus.

So even though the weapon is formed you have to trust God.

II Sam 22:29-37 "For thou art my lamp, O Lord and the Lord will lighten my darkness. For by thee I have run through a troop: by my God have I leaped over a wall. As for God, his way is perfect; the word of the Lord is tried: he is a buckler to all them that trust in him. For who is God, save the Lord? And who is a rock, save or God? God is my strength and power: and he maketh my way perfect. He maketh my feet like hinds feet: and setteth me upon my high places. He teacheth my hands to war; so that a bow if steel is broken by my arms. Though hast also given me the shield of thy salvation: and thy gentleness hath made me great. Thou hast enlarged my steps under me; so that my feet did not slip.

God's design of you being is fearfully and wonderfully made daily. His thoughts of us, and the Master's divine design and creation of us in His imagine meaning nature and character has equipped you so that you will live that II Sam. 22 experience everyday of your life.

My favorite scripture in the bible is Psalm 51:10 *"Create in me a clean heart O God, and renew the right spirit within me.*

I say it all the time when I pray because I realize that God searches the heart of man and I want my heart and thoughts of my heart to be pure towards God. Only those with clean hands and a pure heart can come into the Kings presence.

I was praying and said that scripture with more sincerity one day that I had ever felt before. And the Lord said o.k. here it comes! I was driving home or somewhere I don't remember where, and just like a snap shot or neon sign flashing the scripture

Heb. 12:27, which says "And this word yet once more signifieth the removing of those things that are shaken, as of things that are made, that those things which cannot be shaken may remain.

That blessed me, and as I began to thank God for the experience he said be warned, because 28 and 29 said, *wherefore we receiving a kingdom which cannot be moved, let us have grace, whereby we may serve God acceptably with reverence and godly fear; for our God is a consuming fire*

God is saying in this season that if we will simply surrender the vessel he will perfect

- He will heal it
- He will deliver it out of all manners of bondage
- He will use it
- He will perform his perfect will in it
- He will give each of us direction as to how to take care of the vessel he created.

In order for us to get physically fit and spiritually equipped for the Master's use, we must do something different. We must get understanding of the power that worketh within us.

God gave us grace as a master builder to ready, prepare and sanctify ourselves to be used daily. We are responsible for what we do with and to these temples of the Holy Ghost. No one can say you're too big or too small, or too tall or short or anything of the sort, let a man examine himself. We have to know and prepare ourselves for the assignment on our lives in ministry. We have a blue print for eating right in the bible. Le t your private worship time at home become a physical workout in the worship experience.

Express your song in movement, express your sound in song, express your movement in song. Utilizing physical movement aligns and involves the entire body to participate in the experience. You are an instrument in the Master builder's hands He wants and desires to fine tune.

God gave each of us the favor done without expectation of return to regulate our movement in accordance with that of the heavens and the Father.

In other words let the Holy Spirit that is at work in you teach you all truths, and guide you through your journey and path of life. God gave you this FAVOR, and WISDOM. Why? you say, because once again, "**God gave each of us the favor done without expectation of return to regulate our movement in accordance with that of the heavens and the Father**.

Your purpose and my purpose may not have the same direction, but they do have the same goal. And that is to glorify the father which is in heaven.

God knew and expected you to go through what you've been through to get you where he needed you. So if you are overweight or have some ailments that have kept you from walking in your assignment, seek God in worship and allow him to make his will clear and be still and consecrate your temple until his will is clear. Always operate with wisdom and knowledge, and work it out in your private worship time before the Master.

God anointed and appointed physicians, nurses, and those in the medical field and service to an assignment as well. All things work together", even the gifts and professions. Now having said that if it is the desire of the Father to prosper you, even as your soul prospers, then He (God) is the one that can and will regulate all things to work out for your good. A health or physical challenge can sometimes become that when we compare ourselves to someone else, or try and measure ourselves to someone else, or even allow the situation to become bigger than the God we serve. It creates a dis-ease and can become a disease if it is not dealt with. So instead of claiming it, speak it as a challenge that you can overcome, and conquer by faith and the will of God. Seek the proper help naturally and spiritually, be persistent, and pursuant for victory, because they overcame by the word of their testimony and the blood of the lamb. Instead of asking God why me, what did I do to deserve this, ask this question, what is it you Lord desire I do with this, through this, or in this?.

The bible says "Lift up your heads O ye gates, and be ye lifted up ye everlasting doors and the King of Glory shall come in.

Take a moment and saturate your mind with the full and total 24th Psalm. Just say it over and over until it becomes a melody in your head, and a shield around you. This is a song, allow the melody to come forth out of you that will produce the what, when, where, and why the Lord needs to fortify you with this passage of Psalm. Feel free to dance, move, sing, and create sound to demonstrate your freedom and revelation of this knowledge. Go ahead express yourself!!!!!

As those chosen to lead God's people into His presence we must also lead by example. As a psalmist, minstrel, or minister of movement you MUST be physically fit to endure and withstand the in the natural. You must be able to sing without getting winded and tired after one song. As a minstrel you are required to be able to move your hands and feet without feeling like your body and handle the mobility and mindset to stick to the task. And surely as a dancer you must be able to endure the physical motion and be agile enough to withstand press through to express and demonstrate the sound and song illustrations.

So often we forget we are His instrument of praise. It is God that breathes on you, moves through you and desires to inhabit your praise. Your clapping, stomping, marching, jumping, twirling, and leaping are your worship arsenal. Your vocal cords, limbs and mind are the physical parts of our being that must be fit for the Master's use.

Throughout the bible, the enemies of God's people have been defeated or destroyed by these very movements or worship weaponry. The wall of Jericho came down because they marched around the wall 7 times and shouted. A giant was slain because of what was in the hand of a boy name David. The victory of a battle was won by the worship , and rejoicing of a people outside the territory of an enemy's land, that made them leave the safety of their own home out of fear because of the roar of the worship . Because fear rose in their hearts just by what they heard, and they never laid a hand on them, they simply ushered in the Glory of God into the place where they were. This action caused their enemy to be stricken with fear and trembling and they abandoned the land and all their stuff leaving it behind for the people of God.

The Lord will use what you give him to defeat your enemies. The battle is not yours it is the Lords.

This is the generation that seeks him, that seek thy face O Jacob

Lift up your heads O ye gates and be ye lift up

Ye everlasting doors and the King of glory shall come in

Who is the King of glory? The Lord strong and mighty, the Lord mighty in battle

Lift up your heads, O ye gates even lift them up, ye everlasting doors and the King of glory shall come in

Who is this King of glory the Lord of host, he is the King of glory

(Psalm 24:6-10)

God will fight your battles and endow you with power and strength when you glorify him and invite his glory in. It is our prayer that God will reveal some profound revelation to you about who you are and what wonderful examples of his power have been working through you.

I believe that God is going to reveal some spiritual equipment you may not have had any idea you've been using that have set someone in your family free from bondages of this world.

He'll show you another way to defeat your enemies by just waving your hands in humble submission causing the enemy to flee from you on your job because of your sacrifice of praise. To someone else he'll reveal that every time you clapped your hands or marched in circles and couldn't figure out why you did such an odd thing, (or feel compelled to do such an odd thing)brought deliverance to that son or daughter. He gives you secret weaponry in the words of your song that will release strategies and overcoming power. When we build ourselves up in the word and get greater understanding as to how to apply the word to the physical movement of our temple, to include breathing as well it will afford us a deeper level of wisdom and endowment that can only come from above. The Holy Spirit also has a greater freedom to work on our behalf and speak in proxy for us when the natural body feels as though it can't sing another note, play another chord, or take another step.

As we allow the Holy Spirit to move in us we gain supernatural access to both the spirit realm and the physical manifestation of the power that is already in us.

Now before we begin our physical workout let's take a moment to allow the Holy Spirit to stir in us and activate that connection to the father that dwells in side of each of us as you read the activation scriptures below. Ask the father to surround you with His grace and mercy like a fortress that will be a hedge of protection during this time of vulnerability. And finally a prayer of impartation is released into the atmosphere.

This is an exercise that you can do alone in your private time with the Lord, or with a team or group of people. I really want to admonish you to repeat this action often, because the more you participate in the physical activity the more fit you become for the Master. The more fit you become the more the Master can use you. Get ready get set GO!!!!!

**Challenge

1. Prayer (prayer topic is seeking the Lord for guidance and direction on what you need to do to really get physically fit)
2. Choose at least one scripture from each subject and really commit it to heart as you say it.
3. Seek the holy spirit for creativity of illustration of that scripture in your gift (singing, dancing, or use of instruments)
4.
5. Allow the Holy Spirit to connect the scriptures and gift together that the Lord can speak to you and others through you.
6. Repeat as often as necessary

<u>*FOOD FOR MY SPIRIT*</u>
"SCRIPTURAL ARMOR"

<u>*ARMOR*</u>
EPHESIANS 6:11-18
ROMANS 12:1
ACTS 1:8
AUTHORITY
LUKE 9:1
MATTHEW 18:18
MATHEW 28:19-20
2 CORINTHIANS 10:3-4

BODY BUILDERS
EPHESIANS 2:21-22
ROMANS 8:37
PSALM 47:1
PSALM 51:10
PHILLIPIANS 2:5
ROMAN 8: 27-29
I CORINTHIANS 6:19-20

STRENGTH & POWER
II SAMUEL 22: 29-37
PSALM 149:3-9
FEET
PSALM 56:13
PROVERBS 4:26
PSALM 119:105
HANDS
PSALM 144:1
PSALM 143:6
PSALM 90 16-17
I TIMOTHY 2:8
HEAD
PSALM 24:7-9

(Add more as the Lord Leads you)

Journal question- "What are your scriptures of amour, and why"

_____
_____
_____
_____
_____
_____
_____
_____
_____
_____

Journal question – "What areas are you in need of strengthening"

_____
_____
_____
_____
_____
_____
_____
_____
_____
_____

Session IV
Close Encounter

We are living in such perilous times, and a time of such divination, destruction, and disaster, that is makes me wonder about what we are doing with our praise. If we are to be the salt of the earth, then we should be setting the atmosphere and seasoning the earth with the endowed power we have to be over comers of evil with good, demon busters of destruction, and conquerors of disaster. If when the praises go up blessings come down, there obviously it isn't enough of our praise going up for His blessing to come down. If when we are blessed to be a blessing, then how is it that these things can go on around, and to us during our watch. Psalm 149 gives us an irrevocable illustration of what happens when we praise the King.

(Psalm 149) *Praise ye the LORD. Sing unto the LORD a new song, and his praise in the congregation of saints. Let Israel rejoice in him that made him: let the children of Zion be joyful in their King. Let them praise his name in the dance: let them sing praises unto him with the timbrel and harp. For the LORD taketh pleasure in his people: he will beautify the meek with salvation. Let the saints be joyful in glory: let them sing aloud upon their beds. Let the high praises of God be in their mouth, and a two-edged sword in their hand; To execute vengeance upon the heathen, and punishments upon the people; To bind their kings with chains, and their nobles with fetters of iron; To execute upon them the judgment written: this honour have all his saints. Praise ye the LORD.*

If heaven suffereth violence and the violent taketh by force, then I ask again what are we doing with our praise? God reveals revelation in worship, releases strategies in times of intimacy with him. When we are intimate with our mate something is always produced. A baby is conceived, and deeper fondness for one another is revealed, a closer relationship, and deeper level of love and dependency upon one another.

Only the face to face, or up close and personal encounter could bring such fulfillment. Then the real question becomes, is praise what I do? Or it is an emotional performance?

In the presence of the Lord is fullness of Joy and at His right hand are pleasures for evermore (Psalm 16:11b).

If our praise is so full of faith, hunger and thirst for His righteousness, then isn't it also true to say that we become carriers infected with this joy, righteousness, strategies, power, anointing, and authority to make a difference to have rulership (dominion) in the earth.

If praise is what we do, and we are determined that we walk out Matt.6:33*(But seek ye first the kingdom of God, and his righteousness; and all these things shall be added unto you)* in our praise and our lives then we will see Psalm 149 manifest in our churches, and our communities. Our praise is for the direct pleasure and purpose of the King of kings and Lord of lords. He created us for His good pleasure in His own image, He knows what He likes. It is our duty to present ourselves before the King for that face to face encounter. The father wants you up close and personal. The music, song, movement, and spoken word should always reflect the face of the Master, not just simply be appealing to the eye or ear. It should create an atmosphere that allows His people to see Him through every instrument used. Are we really that generation that will seek His face? Wouldn't it be a marvelous thing to have a worship experience where the Lord enters in and nothing and no one can stand, the priest can't even speak, the preacher, can't preach because the Master is speaking. No song, sound or movement could take place, because such a heavy atmosphere of the Lord was set, that the King of Glory filled the room, stood in the congregation in awe of the aroma of our praise set before Him. Imagine this if you will, that the praise was so pure, and pressing that people on the streets would feel compelled to come in and experience what was going on.

If the worship was so strong and inviting that the hospitals in the vicinity of the praise would find all the people in the hospital rooms miraculously healed and made whole. If the shadow of Peter could bring about such a thing, how much more could an atmosphere of praise and worship do in our time. It is our responsibility, and accountability in the earth to create such a thing, all around the world. We should be seeking the Master's face daily, not just on Sunday and during prayer and bible study night. He is our daily bread, and we do not live by natural bread alone. We also live by every word that proceeds out of the mouth of God. Wouldn't that imply that we are to be up close and personal with the Father? We must be up close and personal to hear His voice. We must be up close and personal to feel His touch. We must be up close and personal and intimate to really know Him. Praise is not a clothing to be put on by the called and set apart. It is the air you breathe, it is the purpose of your existence, and it is the driving force of your life. It is not just intimate to you, it is In-ti-ma-cy (IN TO ME SEE). What does that mean, very simply put, it means what I am, who I am, How am I am, is Him (the Father). Christ Jesus was the perfect example of in-ti-ma-cy. Everything he did reflected the Father, everything he said pointed right back to the Father, wherever he went, He said the Father sent me. Is that our statement, can we say that all that we are doing reflects points back to and is because the Father said this, or sent us.

Shouldn't our songs, sound, and movement (dance, etc.) reflect, and reveal who, and what God is saying to His Bride (the church). If all that the purpose and position we hold makes us look good, and displays are talent and skill, with no real revelatory affect, then what are we doing? Allow and determine that your every breath is to praise Him. Every note and key in sound reflects His heartbeat for His bride. Every step, movement, and instrument displays the beauty of His holiness. We are His joy, and the apple of His eye. Let your praise, worship, and adoration display your heart of gratitude for the honor. Let your heart be filled by the knowledge of who he is takeover your being. He is the lover of our souls.

He is your beginning and your end, He is the air you breathe, take a deep breath and let Him in to a space and a place that only He can touch, ignite, and stir in you that will leave you wanting more.

Now is a good time to meditate on Psalms 51, and allow this to become a song, a dance, a sound, or even a spoken word. As a carrier of His glory, His word should always be the catalyst that propels you into His presence.

In the beginning was the Word, and the Word was with God, and the Word was God (John1:1).

We are the word and our movement, sound, song, and spoken word should be to demonstrate as well as illustrate that principle. God created us for His good pleasure, and as it is His desire for us to draw near to Him, it should be our desire to draw near to Him for a face to face encounter. Does the demonstration of your love, praise, and adoration for the master display that principle without an explanation? Is it easily recognizable to someone that needs to know what that looks like, or is it simply emotional (soulish realm)?

Your praise should invoke someone else to join in, or feel compelled to join in, or usher them into the presence of the Lord simply by the atmosphere of your praise, and adoration that is set before them for Him. The word tells us that only he with clean hands and pure heart can successfully accomplish this. At all times we must purify our hearts, and seek the master according to His plan, not our idea. If no flesh shall glory in his presence then we must check this part of ourselves at all times, especially when we are to go before the King. In the book of numbers the 8th chapter verse 13-15 speaks on the purpose and position of the Levites, which were the chosen carriers of His glory, and the things closest to God's presence to include the Ark of the Covenant , and more specifically the place where they were to be and what they were suppose to do.

(Num. 8:13-15)*And thou shalt set the Levites before Aaron, and before his sons, and offer them for an offering unto the LORD. Thus shalt thou separate the Levites from among the children of Israel: and the Levites shall be mine. And after that shall the Levites go in to do*

the service of the tabernacle of the congregation: and thou shalt cleanse them, and offer them for an offering.

Just as we discussed in one of the earlier sessions we are allowed to be presented before the King, however the King saw you long before you were in the inner courts. What if the King inquired about you on last Tuesday or Wednesday consulting with the Holy Spirit, what would he have seen you doing in representation and preparation for Him. We are carriers of the glory every day. Do a personal examination of the last five days of your activity, and your character. What would it say and would the King of kings be drawn to you even more. As you reflect on the week, I want to remind you that we serve a faithful, loving, merciful God. His word tells us we can come to Him and ask for forgiveness, and He is faithful and just to forgive us. (take some time, while we have the grace and take that thing to the Lord in prayer 1...2...3... GO!!)

Our character, integrity, and motives must be pure in all things, but especially before the people God holds us accountable to show forth His glory. None of us are perfect, and we have all fallen short, but what set the ones pure at heart from the self promoters is a broken and a contrite heart.

The greatest worshipper of all times was David, who was even scribed as a "man after God's own heart" fell short, yet God vowed to rebuild the Tabernacle of David, because it was the place where God promised to dwell forever. David gave his all when it came to the things of God. What will we give? David sacrificed his all for the Lord, will we? Now is the time to purpose in your heart and determine in your mind, that His glory must manifest in the earth through me, as a brick in the wall of the rebuilding of the Tabernacle of David.

A face to face encounter with the Master should be every believer's desire. But you that are set apart for the specific purpose of displaying His glory (the Levites) should move beyond simply having a desire. This is required, and mandated, and should be a yearning, and yielding, and a press to experience. If praise is what you do and you truly seek His face, all I can say is GET READY !!!!!

Take about 45 seconds and simply call on the name of the Lord (All and any of His names, Jehovah Rapha, Jehovah Shalom, etc.) with sincerity, and with a hunger until the essence of His name and character of what is in His name fills your heart with anticipation. From that point illustrate and express back to him what your understanding of what that knowledge means to you personally. Now if you can, be still before him and allow His presence to surround you, and engulf you totally... shhh.

Write this experience down, date it and look back at it at a much later time to see how the growth of your intimacy, and dynamics of your relationship grow and change over time.

This is the point in this manual where you will write more than you read. As you seek the face of the Master there are things that He will reveal to you that the book cannot. There are revelations that the Lord of Host wants to speak to you that I cannot. As you journal and meditate on what is revealed to you, date it and time stamp these truths and unveilings. Each time you go back and reflect on them as the Lord leads you to, ask the Holy Spirit to take you deeper. Select worship, warfare, and music of praise to stir and set the atmosphere for you to truly hear from the Lord. Practice and press your way into this place daily for 7 days consistently and anticipate His presence daily.

"In all thy ways acknowledge God, and He will direct thy path"
(Prov. 3:6)

There is a place that the Master desires to draw you and you alone into. It's another place that has your name on it. It's the place that was designed by the Lord for the face to face encounter planned just for you before the beginning of time. Allow your spirit to hunger and long for that opportunity until you really feel like you can't take it anymore.   Desire the winds of heaven to propel you and even push you into the place of pleasure forever more. Are you longing for His face and absolutely starving for His presence yet?

A face to face encounter with the Master will without a doubt change your life, your view, and your continence that will ultimately shift your ministry.

If you do not or have never considered fasting now would be a good time to seek the Lord as to what kind of fast He is calling you to. Those that is responsible for the things of God, and as a Levite, YOU ARE RESPONSIBLE for the things of God including the preservation and availability of the temple. You must take on the mind of Christ and some things do come by fasting and praying. So often we think a fast is not eating for a certain amount of time. But I would say to you that fasting is a call to consecrate yourself and bring the flesh subject to the spirit by denying the flesh and awakening the spirit to be fed by the word of God, prayer, worship, intimate time spent with the keeper and sustainer of your soul. It is communion, and communication with the redeemer of your soul. Fasting for some is simply food, but I would like to also add that fasting can also be from things including people that can cause you any level of distraction and inability to focus on hearing the voice and command of the Master that can and often cause you to be spiritually anorexic.

That means that you feel like you are alright, but the reality is your spirit and response of your spirit to the Lord is frail. You are really weak, and without strength. Yet you still think that everything is alright. You think all is well but those around you including spiritual leaders concerned about you see your truth and know that you are spiritually unhealthy you really need nourishment from the word or a daily spiritual encounter.

This is a time when preparing yourself for the true presence of the King requires and demands that you do something different in order to receive a different and more excellent way. This is not to say that everything is wrong, out of order, or out of shape. But as so many that the Lord has chosen before you, they too had to prepare themselves for the presence of the Lord and avail themselves to the stretch that is required. ARE YOU READY?

Seeking the Master's face must be serious and intentional. He wants to consume you, and longs for you now. The question is, are you available, and hungry for the fire? I am excited for the encounter you are about to have. Can you feel yourself drawing closer and longing for His touch that makes everything else obsolete? Can you hear his voice and the pulse of His heart in the air?

"And this word, Yet once more, signifieth the removing of those things that are shaken, as of things that are made, that those things which cannot be shaken may remain. Wherefore we receiving a kingdom which cannot be moved, let us have grace, whereby we may

serve God acceptably with reverence and godly fear: For our God is a consuming fire. (Heb. 12:27-29)

Allow the hunger, zeal, and cry of your spirit man to draw you into the place where His glory is revealed, and you see His face. Don't be surprised if you make this discovery on your face at His feet.

Do pull back because it stretches the gift, call and anointing on your life. Don't allow distractions people or things block your entrance into the Holy of holies. Press toward the mark of the high calling which is in Christ Jesus.

Be zealous and unmovable. Seek His face for the encounter your spirit longs for that your flesh can't take. And then once you have obtained this goal go deeper. There a chamber in the Master's secret place that is just for such an encounter for the face to Face experience.

Let Him take you there!!!!!!

Journal question – (you create it by revelation you receive during the intimacy of worship)

_____

_____

_____

_____

_____

_____

_____

_____

_____

_____

_____

_____

_____

_____

_____

_____

_____

_____

_____

Session V
Worship Weaponry

What is worship weaponry, well according to 2 Cor. 10:3-6 it is mighty, and has authority to change not just a world, but nations. It speaks directly to the weaponry and carrier of the weapon having discipline, authority, and accuracy. The word of God in the commentary of the NKJV calls it military discipline. What is the worship weaponry that we carry? Your praise, your worship, travailing in worship, prophetic flow in utterance through song, sound, movement and even prayers are worship weaponry. Every movement, song, and every sound of the instrument, and every praise instrument (tamborette, glory ring, banner, streamer, etc.) have the potential to carry out a militant, strategic and power precision effort for the King of Glory, the Lord of Host. When we study to show ourselves strong, and approved for the Master's use, these things become worship weaponry.

In Psalms 149 it gives us a very specific use as to what we, as instruments in the Master's hand with our praise can accomplish. What if the entire congregation came on what accord for a community, or a specific cause? What if we really come against the wilds of the devil with the whole armor of God on using the instrument of praise, and prayer, while abandoning all other thought and agendas? We are and can be a great arsenal and force to be reckoned with. If everyone's thoughts and focus were all united for that specific purpose and on one accord, they become a wrecking ball. The bible says where just two touch and agree, not only is He in the mist, but also that the thing they agree upon must be established.

In the book of Acts is says *"and they were all with one accord..."* (Acts 2:1)

When there was one mindset the Spirit of the Lord came upon them and filled the whole house, not a few people but all. As a result of that encounter they were all equipped to affect the nations represented outside of those walls and they understood them. That sounds like weaponry to me.

The power of the tongue is very powerful and can be precise in execution like a well sharpened sword. Our songs, exhortation, and exaltation should be used as it were when the walls of Jericho came down.

They were given specific directions, a specific line up, and then a specific charge. As a result of obedience to the command the walls came down and exposed their enemy and gave God's people the victory. The position of the psalmist, minstrel, intercessor, minister of movement and dance is to carry out the front line responsibility as it pertains to praise and worship and that is to bring the walls of discord, distraction, disruption, depression, and division down from amongst the people. It is our responsibility to set the atmosphere by the weapons of our warfare which are not carnal, but mighty through God to the pulling down of strongholds. Our shouts should bring fear and trembling to the enemy's camp. Our claps should pierce and split the eardrums of the enemy. Our sound should cause earthquakes in the earth so much so that is causes everything that would try to exalt itself against the knowledge of God to be shattered.

The purpose of the weaponry is not so we look so militant or powerful, and certainly not for personal gain. It is to be militant and be willing to put our lives on the line in honor of defending our right to worship our God without the tricks and schemes of the enemy as a concern. He is a defeated foe, and we win. When our worship becomes like that of heaven and take our position of praise as a position of power, the God you serve will hide you and Jehovah Nissi "OUR BANNER" rises up over you. When we use the gifts that God has given us to establish and regain dominion in the earth as kings, the kingdom of our Lord advances and overcome darkness.

However, when we do what we are gifted and anointed to do for hire or pay then we otherwise become mercenaries, and the light diminishes. I do agree that you are probably worth your hire as the words says, however if you lend your gifts only to those that can hire you, be careful. Let me put it another way, the world get the training and use it for personal, destructive, or monetary gain only.

If your purpose is to get paid, be put on a pedestal and be recognized, check yourself. When the Kings kids only use the gifts for hire, or only if we are paid or compensated, then we are hirelings or mercenaries. Remember as a Levite he sent you even to the least of them to set the captive free. They ministered before the Lord and were responsible for the things of God to include their talents, time, and treasure. Do not prostitute the gift to the highest bidder. Though the gifts are without repentance, the anointing to operate in power will cost, but only the Master builder can put a price on it. His blood paid for the right to use it. The bible does say and speaks to the fact that when sent, He has already paved your way as "Provider" they'll be taken care of. But when we simply go, you take care of yourself.

What does this mean, glad you asked, because I've been instructed by the Holy Spirit to tell you. When we operate in the will of the Father for our lives then His word says, take no thought for your life. When we seek Him first, He ads ALL other things to our lives. Make sure that when we go, He told us so. When what you do is what He commanded or instructed you to, walk in the steps ordered for you, He will take care of you. God is not a man that he should lie, nor the son of man that he should repent. In other words make sure that we are sent and not just went.

The enemy, Satan, not one another is not happy when we give God praise despite the situation or circumstances we may be facing or going through. The harder and more abandoned we are in our praise to our God, the more confused and upset we can make the enemy in the mist of it all.

The bible speaks of people that caused confusion, and fear to fall on their enemies just from hearing how loud and exuberantly they praised and worshipped their God. They fled from their own land, and the safety of their city because they did not know what was really going on around them, and the physical fight had not even begun. God will give us strategies, songs, hymns, sound, and direction to overcome that very thing that is attempting to overtake us at the precise moment because He knows your enemies could be aiming and attempting to take the fatal blow. But know that no weapon formed against you shall prosper.

We have replaced Satan and his position in the eyes of God concerning praise and worship, and he is pulling out all the stops to keep us from filling the position with power and authority, or even realizing this truth. The question really is do you know who you are, and whose you are and the rights, and privileges and benefits that position comes with this knowing?

The bible in II Timothy talks about studying to show yourself approve. That not only speaks about the word of God, but the craft, and skill training He has given you. Do you attend workshops, classes, conferences, or enhancement courses?

Do you spend time before the Master showing and ministering to Him in your private sanctuary (your home)? Are we like David and look to fill our homes, workplace, and sphere of influence with His presence, creatively, and strategically.

This honor has all the saints!!!!!

Take some time and seek the Master's face to prepare your hands for war and your finger tips for battle "minstrel" To use your voice in the earth and sound the alarm "psalmist". Dancers stir the atmosphere as you spin, leap, clap, and lift up the standard in the banners that show forth and proclaim His name in all the earth. Your feet are as hind's feet, and your arm to break a bow of steel "dancers" of the most High God. Psalmist, declare the word of the Lord in you song, not just the words that sound good, or your prepared song list. Let the Lord use your vocals as a trumpet sounding.

Minstrels play heavens sounds that prepare the way, and blaze trails in the atmosphere for a coming King. We must take up our position, and war for the right to have dominion over all that he said we already have rulership over in Gen.1:26. We are not spiritual cheerleaders, or inspirational motivators. We are designed, created and chosen to go before the Lord in the presence or assembly of the people, not to stir their emotions into a frenzy for the Lord, but their hearts toward Him. Our purpose and assignment is to set the atmosphere conducive for the presence of the Lord our King to enter in.

We are not and should not try and manipulate the atmosphere and order of things to fit what our plan or program needs to make happen. We are the clay and the Lord is the potter, we are in His hands, and should be seeking His face, not a position. Remember your purpose is to be a conduit or outlet, let the Holy Spirit find you connected to the power source and move through you. So often we have the arsenal at our disposal and use it to manipulate the service and experience for our needs and agenda, because it fit the season and time we are in personally. Ecc. 3:1-10 talks about, *to everything there is a time and season.....,* however

Ecc. 3:11 is very specific when it says, *He hath made everything beautiful in its time: also he hath set eternity in their heart, yet so that man cannot find out the work that God hath done from the beginning even to the end.*

We do the work and serve, God gets the Glory. God fights the battle, we get the victory.

The word, and skill build up sharpens the armor, and prepares the warrior. What good is the arsenal if you don't know all that it is capable of? Your armor and your arsenal should not be loaned out or placed just anywhere. Ministers of movement your priestly garments (not costumes) should not be loaned out, shared, or borrowed. A priest never gives out his robes they were made just for him. They are you armor, and should be anointed for the work you do. Take care of them in such a way. Psalmist your voice and body should be cared for and shielded from the elements of the world (a living sacrifice, holy and acceptable). Minstrel your instrument should be taken care of like a soldier cares for his gun, it is personal to him and he knows and is very familiar with every part of it.

We should have a designated place where we meet Him (the Lord), and get daily instructions from Him. But don't misunderstand this point God "is" everywhere. If you don't have a place where you meet God and commune without interruption and alone, find that place of intimacy and make it personal and sacred.

This is sometimes referred to as the chamber, secret place, and yes it can and should be referred to as the upper room. In war it is called the strategy room, or war room, and this room is only open to those of the correct credentials, rank, and position. Others call it a prayer closet, prayer room, or sanctuary. Regardless of what you call it, there should be a private place where you get alone to talk to and hear from the Lord. We are to be armored up and prepared for war. Don't wait to see if someone is on the battlefield, you be the first one, especially if you are the worship leader.

Eph. 6:10-18 tells us the what, why, and who of the war, and what to be prepared for. Are you equipped and ready?

II Sam.22:31-35 says, *"As for God, his way is perfect: The word of Jehovah is tried; He is a shield unto all them that take refuge in him. For who is God, save Jehovah? And who is a rock, save our God?*

God is my strong fortress; And he guideth the perfect in his way.

He maketh his feet like hinds' feet, And setteth me upon my high places.

He teacheth my hands to war, So that mine arms do bend a bow of brass".

The chords of the instruments, the words in a song, the steps and movements of a dancer, and the instruments of banners, streamers, etc, are simply the tool, you are the instrument. *The weapons of our warfare are not carnal, they are mighty through God to the pulling down of strongholds (2Cor. 10:4).*

There should be an iron sharpening iron experience during your rehearsal and preparation time. The psalmist gift and arsenal of songs should sharpen the ear of the minstrel to shift in the realm of the spirit in places unknown. The minister of dance or movement should be able to propel the psalmist into realms in the spirit that bring forth the songs that take authority of the atmosphere. Each of these entities should be capable of stirring one another and shifting one another dimensionally, the sound to song, the song to sight, and the sight to sound.

We must know the purpose and strategies of the Master and what to do effectively in order to follow through on the plan set before us, and the direction necessary to overcome the enemy. We can and should be just as affective in our homes and our church, workplace, and assignments around the world. Our communities, families, and neighborhoods should be changed by what and how we prepare ourselves in the hands of the Lord.

Every warrior chosen and set apart should know the original intent of the gifts within us as it lines up with the word. We should study and seek the word daily for the direction of the Lord as He desires to prepare us daily for the assignment on our lives. If you are a minstrel, then you are not just a minstrel on Sunday, you are created to be that daily. You should be looking to make melody, and music all day for the Lord. You should hear tempo, crescendo, rhythm, and beats in the very air and atmosphere around you. Psalmist even when you are speaking and having a conversation, there should be a command and leadership quality about your voice that draws others to you and make them want to listen to you and be encouraged by your very presence. As a dancer, every step you take should potentially be a step of authority everywhere you go. All of this should be like breathing, you don't think about it, it simply is.

Do you know what the Greek and Hebrew terms of praise, worship, sound, song, and dance mean? How does it apply to you individually? Do you know how to originate and interpret the word in Greek and Hebrew for what you do? What does the bible say about your individual gift, and calling? Has the Lord shown you what your specific anointing is for and given you a direct scripture in His word to confirm that? We should know the original intent of the gift, skill, or talent we operate in. We should know the language, vocabulary and understanding of what we do and why as an individual are we charged with being a carrier of His glory. The word tells us to study to show ourselves approved.

We are required to know and give attention to the word, which is not just the truth of the matter, but the reality, wisdom, knowledge, and totality of living under and through the word. How can we know Him, except we spend time learning of Him.

Seek him while He may be found. Yearn for Him, thirst after His righteousness, and seek Him diligently. When we discover more about Him, we find out more, and unveil more of who we are. Study and do something daily to increase your skill level, training and understanding of the purpose and call on your life. God has not purposed and equipped us and called us to do the work without realizing that, to whom much is given, much is required. We must spend time daily seeking His face, and studying to show ourselves approved. If you are a musician, spending time in His presence, and specifically in his face, He will change your position from musician to minstrel. If you are a singer, spending time in His face He will change your songs to that of the psalmist. If your position is a dancer, seeking His face will allow you and afford you the opportunity and authority to be called and assigned the purpose of your dance to speak and demonstrate the message of the Master and become a minister of movement. So I ask the question again, will this be the generation that will seek His face?

So often we want to look holy, and have a form of godliness, and denying the power therein, but I dare say that the body of Christ does not need any more musicians, singers, or dancers that operate under the guise of praise teams or choirs that sit in positions to usher the people of God into His presence. We need minstrels, psalmist, and ministers of dance or movement to break forth and operate in power, and anointing to destroy the yokes, set the captive free, and break up the fallow ground, so that the word of God, and the saturation of His presence moves through to edify His people and build them up.

In order to define these positions with power to operate at full capacity, I challenge you to discover the skill and training that will thrust your gift into the now season for prophetic flow, intercession, warfare, travail, restoration, deliverance, healing, and much, much, more. Once again journal these progressive steps, date them and move from glory to glory as the Lord leads you.

As the descriptions and refined purpose of your arsenal gets sharpened, share the good news with those on the front line with you. Believe God for strategic placement and understanding of those on the line with you. Become the greatest intercessor for your ministry, your community, your home, family and friends.

Watch God promote you to a status of general because He can trust you with the best of His weaponry His people.

The close encounter, face to face experience puts you in the place and position to receive the strategy and inside information from the Master.

What has your close encounter revealed? And more importantly have you had one?

**Journal question
What is the purpose and power of your gift and anointing?

_____

_____

_____

_____

_____

_____

_____

_____

_____

_____

_____

_____

_____

_____

_____

_____

_____

_____

_____

_____

Session VI
"The Moved Word"

For so long dance, music and song have been used in so many places that we can no longer recognize its original intent, as it pertains to the body of Christ and worship unto the Lord. The distortion of the world's use and depiction of dance, music and songs in videos, television, sports and commercials, etc., has caused the church to frown upon the need specifically of dance and some instruments in the sanctuary of God across our great nation and the world. This debate and misinterpretation has belittled the power and atmospheric grace and authority of praise and worship. God in his infinite wisdom created us in his own likeness, and then he empowered us to usher in his presence through the instrument of the body in movement, with song and sound. He desires that earth looks like heaven, because the Kingdom of heaven must come to the earth, so that the fullness of his will is done on earth as it is in heaven.

The creative sounds and use of instruments that glorify God have long since the beginning of time been debatable, and an argument in some churches. Dance was created by God for the displaying of his Holiness through movement. Some instruments to include dance have been excluded from the church and worship experience because of the negative association they have to being provocative, and alluring. We have allowed the continuous misinterpretation of these tools to now become the defined purpose and use. The church feels better when these gifts are left in the world. Satan danced, sang, and played the instruments upon himself and congregation of angels joined him. We are responsible for the restoration of all things created to bring God glory back to the body of Christ. We are to correct and charge the atmosphere on earth as it is in heaven and around the throne. We have accepted every manner of alteration and distortion to come in because we like it and it makes us feel good, without really seeking the Master and laying the matter before the King.

We dress it up and call it hip hop praise, youthful praise, worship with a twist, etc. If it draws attention to the person or invokes the thoughts of the flesh, then the presenter needs redirect the focus, and check their own motives of the movement and music.

Satan was the original praise and worship leader, the Lord put him in a prestigious position and even placed all the instruments and sounds in him that please him (the Lord). Satan was able to cause a movement so great in heaven the he lured a third of the angels to be captivated by all that he was doing. He was self motivated, stimulated, and illuminated. Because he felt equal to God and worthy of the right to the praise and attention, and the position, he became blinded and self absorbed in his own stench. Has your position and the words you sing, speak, or display in movement or sound caused you to move the people, or His glory through you move the people into His presence. When Lucifer thought to high of himself and his ability to move and stir the other angelic beings, God fired him and sent those that followed him with him. As a result of this act, to this day the church and those that God created for His good pleasure still believe that dance and, all that loud sound is only for the world and that heaven is some quiet place that angels whisper holy, holy, holy......

Let's talk about what happens when we dance, or become the word in movement, or declare the sounds and songs of heaven here on earth as a part of the experience of setting the tone and atmosphere for praise and worship. Look at Psalms 149:3, it talks about what you are doing in the mist of the dance, it speaks of binding the enemy (Psalms 149: 7-9), and subduing him with the very thing that he has bound the people with (chains & iron). The movement interprets the word, it displays the word, and it illuminates the word of God and the songs and melody unto the Lord to set his people free to praise, worship, and glorify him with an abandoning liberty. Dance in the world draws the attention and focus to the person dancing because of the movement of the body. It can be suggestive, provocative, and lustful to the eye. It is considered to be entertaining, and a performance.

In the world it can be attention seeking by the dancer and self promoting (look at me!!) from the audience to capture their thoughts and is sometimes considered hypnotic, or hypnotizing.

However, dance in the church is a tool used to draw attention, direction, and focus to the Lord Jesus Christ. It is the dancer's obligation and responsibility to the Lord to surrender everything for his purpose. You must begin with your mind, then your body and subsequently your actions both in the church and outside the church. Why, because your body is the temple of the Holy Ghost, and you are the church that is deemed to operate both in and outside the walls of the building. The dancer must become a living sacrifice, and empty. The vessel cannot draw the focus or thoughts of the people towards him or herself. This is accomplished by having your thoughts, body, and movement totally under the direction given over to the Holy Spirit through constant prayer and an attentive ear to hear.

In reference to the music, melody, and lyrics, there is really no variable difference as we described the example in the movement aggregate. When the sound and song cause or create erratic chords, and lyrics provoke ill will, thoughts and behavior or even give excuses for erratic behavior tempered and hidden and shrouded with the misinterpretation of the word, then it can do just as must damage as the movement in manipulation. When the lyrics provoke thoughts of flesh and self promotion, God is not pleased. When the sound mimics the sound of the world and puts the people in remembrance of a song or sound of the earth it is wrong and not of God.

Those that have accepted and operate in the charge of the Levitical priesthood have a responsibility and duty to be carriers of His glory and move according to His plan and not fulfill our own need to be seen, heard, or put on a pedestal. Remember that's how Lucifer got fired.

Let's take a moment and ask the Holy Spirit to direct the activity of our limbs and our actions vocally and musically to display his holiness that pleases him. Ask the Holy Spirit to direct and move in and through you, while hiding you in Him. Use Psalm 91 as a blue print and muse. Sincerely seek His plan for your movement, vocally, musically, and physically that he wants to set in

Min. Que. Payne

the atmosphere according to the power working within you of Him.

Remember dance is used to draw the people into the presence of the Lord through the illumination of movement of the song, spoken, and musically directed presentation via spontaneous movement, worship, or praise. The sight, sound or song can ignite an atmosphere, for warfare, intimate worship before the Father, deliverance, or even healing. The components of sight, sound, and song must and should work in conjunction with each other to create the majestic and melodic flow in and on the earth as it is in heaven. Each one was designed to cover and command a strategic realm in the spirit that they need one another to operate, but can operate as an individual entity. The dancer becomes the instrument, the lyrics illuminate the word of God, and the sound sets and affects the atmosphere. Dancing in the church, or temple is a stirring up of the Holy Spirit and a universal language set to invoke the presence of the Lord to effectually consume the people for his glory. Typically the psalmist are platformed or stand in the pulpit while the minstrels can be set even higher behind, beside, and even stationed on the main flooring area which is where the charge of the movement is conducted with and without instruments (banners, streamers, flags, etc.) However there are no set patterns or positioning.

All dance, songs, and sound in the world is not bad or provocative, it just does not usher in the presence of the Lord and meant for the church. Dance such as ballet, tap, modern dance, and social line dances are not necessarily negative or bad by nature. Sound and song genres of other diversities are not all derogatory. Religious dance, sound and songs go back to early biblical times of the Israelites.

They danced with and without music for their victories, for celebrations of events such as weddings, wars, mourning, and births. Music and various instruments were used from the beginning of time for various reasons and purpose. These various uses were designed to inspire, invoke, and provoke many different responses and not all negative or demonic.

I Sam. 18:6, II Sam. 6:14, are a few examples of dance and variations of purpose of the dance. The entire book of psalms were written as songs and used and depicted various stories of the times. They speak of war, worship, declarations, exaltations and much more. Music was even used to sooth and calm the king (Saul). David was a young man and the king (Saul) ask that David come and play the instrument to sooth him of the evil spirits that were tormenting him. (See I Sam. 16:1-23)

They danced and sang songs to praise and glorify God for every occasion (Ps. 30:11, Ps. 150)

Kings and priest in early times used music and songs to proclaim an ordinance, proclamation or command before the people. Music was used to give instructions and directives to the soldiers in war, etc. It was a call to order, it was used to announce the coming or entrance of the king and the courts of the king.

Dance, music, and song are praise and worship tools used to activate the spirit and admonishes the people to praise God, and welcomes the Holy Spirit into the sanctuary for the uniting of the congregation for corporate rallying to operate on one accord. Songs and lyrics can and does bring the people into the corporate and unified mindset to set their thoughts and heart toward the Lord. The use of all of these components should and will connect the congregation and will usher the people into the His inner court to receive what He has for them, and what He wants them to hear from Him. You are to assist and serve the house and Pastor/Shepherd of the house for the delivery of the word.

** Close your eyes and ask the Holy Spirit to guide you and give you a creative flow demonstrating in your perspective gift and calling using II Chron. 7:14 to set the atmosphere for, *Psalms 16:11 " THOU WILL SHEW ME THY PATH OF LIFE: IN THY PRESENCE IS THE FULLNESS OF JOY; AT THY RIGHT HAND ARE PLEASURES FOR EVERMORE* to be loosed in the earth by your anointing and gifts.

Dance, music, and song or psalms in the church help to set the atmosphere for His people to receive joy, peace, salvation, healing, deliverance, restoration, and so much more. In the presence of the Lord nothing is impossible. Mass miracles can take place. A spontaneous or prophetic song or word can be released from the throne room of God (like an instant e-mail) because worship is an automatic response when the presence of the Lord fills a room. These skills work in conjunction with one another along with, the prayers, and the spoken word to effectually illuminate it's power and purpose.

These are also instruments that can and was created to assist and aid in the setting of the atmosphere for such a move of God to take place, through the ministry of dance, sound, and song. You are the carrier of His glory with a message on the inside of you for His people. Count it a privilege and an honor to be chosen by the Lord to be a Psalms 150 vessel.

Aren't you ready to see the miracles signs and wonders not just follow after you, but overtake you and the entire congregation. It is time to move into the realm of the miraculous. The world is dying because the people of God won't move in the realm of the spirit that releases the true power of God's presence.

Will you dare to be set apart and peculiar, and not care about how someone else views you? We need to seek HARD after God and not quit until we have obtained HIM and the manifestation of His Glory COMES ALIVE in us.

We should desire to come before His presence naked and unashamed. When we surrender totally things change. When you sing and declare the word of the Lord, it shall come and move on the people and it should hit you first. Why, because you have a zeal and passion for Him like Jacob did.

We shall receive a name change as a result then they (God's people) will receive the glory of God through your experience and choice to be used as a vessel for God to fill up and pour out. When the minstrel plays the sounds that will cause his or her own heart to repent and cry out and not care whether they talk about you or not, but allow them to see you broken then He will become a conduit for the cry of the people to break forth. When the minister of movement and the instruments wave the flag until their own deliverance comes forth or dance until healing breaks forth in your own body from ailments and infirmities then and only then can and will the groans of the earth be fulfilled and spring forth the seed of healing for the people. You are the seed that the earth is pregnant with. Break forth and move in the earth in all that you are. Spring forth with new songs that you hear the angels cry out as you hear the Lord whisper intimately in your ear. Don't be afraid to take the leap in your dance, create that new instrument. Sing the song of Zion the will cause mass healings to take place. WE MUST STOP PRETENDING!!

WE HAVE TO BE THE SALT OF THE EARTH NOW BEFORE OUR SAVOR RUNS OUT.

We are becoming diluted by our own pride, arrogance and self absorption. He is looking for those that have the songs in their belly that deliver the message of the Master not just to the masses, but also to the one. Come and sit at the Master's feet and receive the download of the in time word for a right now NEED. We do not need another song to tickle the ear. We do not need another dance to wow and entertain us. We do not need another musician to come and show the world your skills and fabulous chords that can sooth and who them and not move them to change.

ENOUGH IS ENOUGH!!!!

Allow the Lord and the moving of the Holy Spirit to use you by totally surrendering the vessel to be a living sacrifice, Holy, and acceptable unto God, which is your reasonable service (Rom. 12:1).

I believe that God wants all his children to receive the fullness of his presence. We are being hoodwinked and lost in the cause by our own need to move the crowd, and have lost the focus of exalting Him. We have to come back to our first love of the calling on our lives. We must go back to the place where we first received and heard the call to come before Him and lend you gift to the ushering in of His presence. As a Levite you are offered up and charged to give thanks and exhortation unto the Lord before the people.

To truly redefine a sincere passion for His presence, we must be willing to allow His word to move on our hearts and break us again. You must surrender to him your all, all of your mind, all of your strength, your whole heart, your body, and your talents. If the word cannot and does not move you, don't expect the word to move through you by the spirit.

God is spirit; they that worship him must worship him in spirit and in truth (John 4:24).

We often hide ourselves in our gifts because we get from others what we need to feel validated. This is not a position where we can hide and think that our Lord does not see our true motive, He does not look at the flesh. Your heart and spirit will show who you really are to the Master and sometimes the people. Those that are called must not be moved by their comments, and accolades. We are responsible as glory carriers to give all honor and glory to Him that has sent us.

Now this is a very touchy subject and area, because the sound and song (psalms) as is the word of God was with our Lord from the beginning. Lucifer was the totality of sound and song in heaven that the Lord created to be pleasing to himself, and be a constant endless source of His praise. Well we all know the story of how Lucifer messed up and thought more highly of Himself than he ought to, so has some of the musicians and psalmist and ministers of movement that are set and released in the church and the industry of music.

It should be noted that it is a dangerous position to put yourself in to think that the service or atmosphere is set when you play, sing, or dance. What you do and how well you think you do it should hold the congregation or the body of Christ hostage or beholden to you, remember they are His people. If you feel like the service begins and ends with you, be aware. Pride goeth right before a fall. Lucifer got caught up in the sounds that flowed through him and began to listen to what was flowing through him and even taking in the way the angels responded to him, to be for him . It was through him and NOT to him. He losing sight of that fact is what got him terminated and permanently removed from the position. When Lucifer was kicked out of heaven God changed his name, but nowhere in the word did it say He (the Lord) removed what was in him (Satan). I believe when he was sent to earth he planted a few seeds, chords, moves and sounds on the earth of his own to capture the minds and ministry of those God would choose to replace him. We have to be careful of the platform we stand on does not become our own pedestal of arrogance, and self absorption.

Music, movement and song have an aroma that can and does induce a certain sensory perception in the air. Hard rock can cause a sense of anger, frustration, tension, etc., in the air. Jazz can create a soothing, mellow, sense in the atmosphere. We see the affects, of rap, blues, and so on and so forth you get the picture, they aren't all necessarily bad just not for his glory. Yet we want to make the music, songs and movement in the sanctuary that are suppose to glorify his name to be like, sound like and become just as the world with a few well place changes . The world moves and tickles the emotions (entertain and perform). The sound, sight and song in the body of Christ is for His glory and should be executed for Him, to Him, for them to see Him and the spirit connection for inspiration to seek after Him. The heart, not just the skill of the musician comes through the sound and tones they set. The difference between a minstrel, and a musician and a singer and a psalmist is not skill, it is the anointing plus heart equal submission to reproduce the sounds of heaven, not just melody, and pitch.

So a man thinks in his heart so he is. The sound is the unspoken word of God that operates in a dual realm earth (natural) and heaven (spiritual). The question is where does your sound come from, who is it for, and what are the intentions? Is it for and released only for pay, power, and prestige, or His pleasure, His purpose and His praise.

We must all be willing to examine ourselves and be open to except what is the truth of the matter. Remember they that worship him, must worship him in spirit and in truth. (John 4:24)

The Holy Spirit comes to reveal and show us all truths.

I would like to suggest a formula I found that works and I continue to use:

Step 1. Pray
Step 2. Repent
Step 3. Receive His forgiveness
Step 4. Praise Him
Step 5. Worship Him
Step 6. Be Still
Step. 7 Obey Him
** Repeat steps as necessary**

Every part of our being was meant to invoke the presence of the Lord to maximize our potential of movement. Remember in Him we move breath and have our being. Let's break down the temple to understand the purpose and power we can operate in.

From the crown of or head to the tips of our toes you are purposed by design to show forth His glory. As we move naturally something spiritual takes place. You do not have to be a trained dancer to operate in power, just a submitted vessel, although formal training isn't a bad idea. You don't necessarily have to be a skilled musician, or psalmist(although some knowledge and training helps).Time and time again we have seen in the word of God that even the most versed and educated were not always God's choice. He chooses according to the how we avail ourselves, and long for Him. We must come broken and have a pure in heart. God is seeking after those that are hungering and longing after Him, His righteousness, and His Kingdom.

Give in to His call, surrender your all. If He is Lord, then He already has ownership (Lord means owner, or ruler).

So, your crown (head) covers mind, intellect, thought center or headquarters. "Let this mind be in you that was also in Christ Jesus". "You anoint my head with oil". Christ is the head of the church submit and surrender you thought to His authority (Christ) and allow His thoughts to be your thoughts, and His ways your ways. Your arms, and hands have power beyond measure. If you trust the Lord and allow him to direct your path, He then releases power and strength upon us that enables us to break a bow of steel with our arms (II Sam.22:35) penetrate unseen realms with our sound, and charge the atmosphere with direction with our words. Even your fingertips have power in the Lord for His purpose NOT your boast. Your Legs, and your feet have untapped potential purpose and power. The Lord will even keep you from stubbing your toe. God truly created your being for His good pleasure. And finally the light of the Master illuminates the anointing not you, for His glory.

Take a moment and use every part of your being including the breath in your body to display His holiness and exalt His name and praise Him with all of your strength, and all of your might. There is about to be a shift in the spirit as you move naturally, Let the Lord move you in the spirit as well. Seek his word (the bible) to find out and discover the foundation of your individual calling and the power by His word to empower and propel you to another place in Him. Afterwards take notice of what the Lord has done on your behalf. As you study and meditate on that word allow the power of the Holy Ghost to move through you, for you, and without question in you. Sing, dance, pray, or play the instrument of gifting in your hands as you read Psalm 24.

(Don't forget to journal).

The more you surrender the more the Lord can and will do on your behalf even to and for generations after you.

Movement literally can change the atmosphere around you to affect the circumstances and situations that take place in, around and to our lives and the lives of those we love. Ask yourself what atmosphere has movement, music, and song stirred up in you through you and to you lately?

We can either stir and affect the atmosphere around us, or sit back and watch it move around us. Either way someone or something is affecting, or infecting it. We have the power and presence of the Lord (the owner and ruler) with us to work it all out for our good.

If He has called you then, He has equipped, justified, and empowered you to make a difference at home, at school, the marketplace, you community, your church, the world. *"The Earth is the Lord's, the fullness thereof, the world and they that dwell therein. (Ps.24:1)*

But He gave us dominion and rulership over the function on the earth. It is now required and commanded that we take the gospel into all the earth. In order to affect the entire world, we must be fit for the Master's use. Even as the Lord taught and trained the disciples for their assignment, so He desires to do so to us and through us. His word says, greater works shall we do. Just as an athlete prepares and trains, we are required to do the same. It is marathon time and the Olympics are upon us. Those who minister in movement, song, or sound, must study and allow the Holy Spirit to guide and direct all movement, sound, and song. And just as the message of the preacher must be based on the sure foundation of the word, we must do the same preparation and seek the same foundation.

If in the beginning was the word, and the word was with God and the word was God, we are representatives or ambassadors of that same premise. *Know that we are not our own, but the temple of the Holy Ghost.* You must feed yourself the enriched substance of the word daily. Dine from the table of the Master that is full of power provoking delicacies. Have a discipline and determination that circumstances, challenges, and situations around you don't move you or deter you from this mission and mandate.

Sometimes as we are in between the course servings, you must marinate or meditate on what you have already been served. Have you taken the time to reflect upon what delights He has already provided? If not I dare you to take a moment and look back on all the delightful meals you have already feasted upon just this past week alone. What has the Holy Spirit served you, what has the Lord of Host fed you personally? What rare treats have you experienced in worship this week, last week, yesterday? *"Oh taste and see that the Lord is GOOD!!!*

After dining at the table of the Master it now becomes the assignment of all who were at the table to tell someone else about the feast. That could be by ministry of movement, song, sound, or the preached word or perhaps just a word of encouragement and your testimony. Because we serve a God that is creative beyond measure, remember He created the earth and all the things in it from shear desire to see it become. What more can we create in reverence of who he is to display our hearts of gratitude and spirit of delight to His majesty. God has given us creative ingenuity to develop and set the atmosphere not just for His presence, but also for others to experience what you know.

When we dance, sing, preach, or play an instrument for the purpose of his presence it must be for His glory, and not our own, it must be to invoke His presence and not people to our position.

We are the clay He is the potter. Be moldable, and easy to handle in the Master's hands.

Journal question- " What was revealed to you in the 7 step process"

_____

_____

_____

_____

_____

_____

_____

_____

_____

_____

_____

_____

_____

_____

_____

_____

_____

_____

VII
Positioned with Purpose

To everything there is a season, a time for every purpose under heaven(Ecc.3:1)
This scripture has been quoted numerous times and used to support so many theories about life and things we aspire to do. We can all relate to this scripture because it's true, there is a time and season for everything. Sometimes we want the season and the thing, but in our time, not necessarily God's timing. Perhaps that's why he said in the verse 11 *He has made everything beautiful in its time.* He *has put eternity in their hearts, except that no one can find out the work that God does from beginning to end.*

I believe that God has a strategic work plan for each of us and only He knows when the timing and seasons are perfectly lined up with us and in the right position to carry out that assignment at that time. We are not to be anxious for anything, but with prayer and supplication make you request known. He also told us to pray , *"Thy will be done".* When we pray the Father's will and submit to that He will make all things beautiful in its time. Sometimes we want what seems as though we are ready for, not realizing the time is not yet right. We can feel it, we know it is close, but is it right, and is it right now. There is a tribe that is spoken of, the tribe of Issachar, who knew the times, and what to do.

I Chron.12:32, "And of the children of Issachar, men that had understanding of the times, to know what Israel ought to do, the heads of them were two hundred; and all their brethren were at their commandment".

The Lord is calling for us to have the spirit of Issachar. We must know the times with understanding, and what to do. Not just to overcome for a moment, but to overtake in this season. Our songs, sound, dance, etc., must be power filled, anointed, and called for the time at hand. In other words we must be in the correct position, in order to hear correctly, and operate accordingly. We cannot do church business as usual, and act like nothing is wrong. There is a protocol, and an order to everything.

We must submit to leadership, and understand the proper protocol of the positions. As there were from the beginning of time, so it should be now in the house of God. We have been given a level of accountability. We are all subject to the house and should flow in the position we have been assigned, not the one we feel we could do better than the one currently in the position of our desire. Your gifts will make room for you. God requires that we do things decent and in order. We serve a God of order. The children of Israel, had to follow a certain order when they left out of Egypt. The twelve tribes were set in a specific place at the gates, and camped around the temple in a designated position.

And so here we are today being positioned for His presence. Can you here Him giving you the placement and the lineup.

Eph 4:10-12,He that descended is the same also that ascended far above all the heavens, that he might fill all things.)And he gave some to be apostles; and some, prophets; and some, evangelists; and some, pastors and teachers; for the perfecting of the saints, unto the work of ministering, unto the building up of the body of Christ:

When Christ position changed He changed ours. Within the ranks are positions of strategy, each with a specific function and purpose. If you are a minstrel, and have been given the mantle of the Apostle, then operate in the area you have been given charge to cover. Set order, and develop those called and need to be set properly.

If you are a dancer, and have the anointing of the Prophet, then minister in the function and flow in what you are. Become the oracle of God in your movement, that encouragers and speaks wisdom and knowledge. We must all do the work in which we all called to do as the body, and stop trying to be the head. Christ is the head, and we must and can only operate as the body. Our ministry work may have us in dual positions, however, that does not mean mine and yours simply because I like what you do better, and feel I can do it better. If I am a hand, then I must function in the position and placement given the hand. It would look quite strange if the foot was in the place of the arm. Or the fingers where the toes flow and go.

Our praise and worship and setting of the atmosphere for the King of Glory, can only be done effectively with power and purity when we all flow and function in the position that has been assigned to us from the Holy Spirit. As a dancer, illustrate the beauty of His holiness in your movement, and even your garments. As a minstrel, create the atmosphere of the sweet melodies that please the Master and show forth His splendor. As a psalmist declare His greatness in song and lyric that will describe His deity with power. When all these position are operating in full power and not separate or apart from one another we create a picture on earth even as it is in heaven. Can you imagine the aroma set in a room when we all have the same goal in mind, with an unquenchable thirst for His presence that we all refused to allow anything else to distract us from. We become the picture of heaven described in Revelation chapter 4. Even the animals, and nature itself will yield to. We have been given charge and dominion over every creeping thing that creeps upon the earth.

(Psalm 24)The earth is Jehovah's, and the fullness thereof the world, and they that dwell therein. For he hath founded it upon the seas, And established it upon the floods.

Who shall ascend into the hill of Jehovah? And who shall stand in his holy place?

He that hath clean hands, and a pure heart; Who hath not lifted up his soul unto falsehood, And hath not sworn deceitfully. He shall receive a blessing from Jehovah, And righteousness from the God of his salvation. This is the generation of them that seek after him, That seek thy face, even Jacob. Selah

Who is the King of glory? Jehovah strong and mighty, Jehovah mighty in battle.

Lift up your heads, O ye gates; Yea, lift them up, ye everlasting doors: And the King of glory will come in.

Who is this King of glory? Jehovah of hosts, He is the King of glory. Selah

If every minstrel, every psalmist, every dancer, every bearer of the streamers, and banners would take up their position on the front line and before the alter of God, displaying their sincere hearts cry for the full manifest presence of God to the place and His people we would experience II Chron. 7:14 across the earth.

We must and now have no choice but to seek His face to learn and fulfill the position for His presence to manifest. If we really took the time to study and seek the Lord concerning the placement, and purpose of our position, God is faithful, kind, and merciful enough to allow us the opportunity to get it right. John 4:24 claims this to be our truth.

He is looking for us to be in position, and receive of Him in the areas He has given us to operate in.

Take some time right now and call on Him. Take some time right now and give Him praise for another chance. Take some time right now and lay before the Lord and allow Him to properly place you. Are you ready? Can you hear Him? Get Prepared for the King. He is looking for a prepared people.

Are you in the right position for His presence?

And so now that you have prayed and declared the call and election as your truth and availed yourself as a vessel prepared for the master. Now that you have been assured of the season of preparation, and desire to be fit for the Master seeking His face and sharpening the weaponry of your worship, move in the message of your ministry. You are prepared, positioned, and purposed with power.

I speak over you a constant joy, hunger, zeal, and passion for His presence, no matter what the cost. I declare that all that the Lord God almighty has need of and has fully equipped you with comes forth without hesitation, holdback, or setback in Jesus name.

I decree and declare that you are one of the ones that will and has been seeking His face, and the encounter and time you have spent in the intimate place and chamber with the lover of your soul has produced much seed of prosperity, righteousness, endless love and wealth to your soul, you ministry, your purpose, and your life in its entirety without lack. I speak that because of who you are and the revelation of whose you are that He the Lord God almighty shall always hold you close and keep you. In Jesus name and by the blood I pray that he will always be your first love and you always acknowledge in as your cover, keeper, protector, shield and banner.

Be blessed in your constant pursuit of His glory, and endowed with His everlasting love.

Lord it is my personal desire and prayer that all the new songs of heaven that have been written, all the new sounds that only a heavenly encounter could reveal be released in Jesus name. All the new and creative movements in dance and instruments showed forth the beauty in holiness that set the captive free be released in Jesus name, by the blood of the lamb.

Lord I pray that all of your people that have shared in this journey are all the better equipped for the work at hand in ministry, life, and examples bring others into your presence, everywhere that you send them not because they received this information, but because they have receive so much of you that you have allowed and afforded us the opportunity to share in as well, in all of the earth let your glory be revealed.

May he keep you and shine over, in, and through you ALWAYS IN JESUS NAME!!!!

All of this is....... FOR HIS GLORY

Journal question- " Who are you in Christ Jesus"

_____
_____
_____
_____
_____
_____
_____
_____
_____
_____
_____

Journal question – "What is your purpose"

_____
_____
_____
_____
_____
_____
_____
_____
_____
_____

Journal question- "What is your position"

_____
_____
_____
_____
_____
_____
_____
_____
_____
_____
_____
_____
_____
_____
_____
_____
_____
_____

LETTER OF COMMITMENT TO THE MASTER

Write a letter of commitment to the Father as to what you will agree to do in ministry from this day forward. These words are a vow as in marriage to the groom (the Lord) from you His bride.

****STOP*****

Before you continue prepare yourself for this encounter in private or as a ministry team as a time of intimacy and sincerity

THIS WILL BE YOUR WEDDING DAY CREATE IT AS SUCH FOR A MEMORIAL IN YOUR HEART